The Witches' Almanac

Spring 2021—Spring 2022

CONTAINING pictorial and explicit delineations of the
magical phases of the Moon together with information about astrological
portents of the year to come and various aspects of occult knowledge
enabling all who read to improve their lives in the old manner.

The Witches' Almanac, Ltd.

Publishers   Providence, Rhode Island
www.TheWitchesAlmanac.com

Address all inquiries and information to
THE WITCHES' ALMANAC, LTD.
P.O. Box 1292
Newport, RI   02840-9998

13-ISBN: 978-1-881098-76-8 The Witches' Almanac—Classic
13-ISBN: 978-1-881098-74-4 The Witches' Almanac—Standard
E-Book 13-ISBN: 978-1-881098-75-1 - The Witches' Almanac—Standard

ISSN: 1522-3184

First Printing July 2020

Printed in USA

Established 1971 by Elizabeth Pepper

Preface

Celebrating a year of the Sun, we have much to be looking forward to. Although we go through periods of pain and strife, there is always a light at the end of a trial. Sometimes it is resolution; sometimes it is the wisdom of the experience.

It is apparent that in a world of health concerns, social unrest and financial instability, society begins to question where we are and where we are going. Well, it is always important to know where we are. Where we are going is a matter of where we would like to be. As Witches and magicians, we have choices. And, these choices come from opportunities that are spawned from change. We must never stay in a state of stagnation or dis-ease. We strive to make ourselves stronger and the world an improved place. Opportunities don't rise up from the wells of comfort and lethargy.

A Witch knows how to ride the strong wind and land in fertile soil, as opposed to clinging on to the rock so as not to be moved by the wind. Accept change. Seize your power. Embrace the wind. *Ad astra per aspera*!

HOLIDAYS

Spring 2021 to Spring 2022

March 20 . . . . Vernal Equinox
April 1 . . . . All Fools' Day
April 30 . . . . Walpurgis Night
May 1 . . . . Beltane
May 8 . . . . White Lotus Day
May 26 . . . . Vesak Day
May 29 . . . . Oak Apple Day
June 5 . . . . Night of the Watchers
June 21 . . . . Summer Solstice
June 24 . . . . Midsummer
July 23 . . . . Ancient Egyptian New Year
July 31 . . . . Lughnassad Eve
August 1 . . . . Lammas
August 13 . . . . Diana's Day
August 17 . . . . Black Cat Appreciation Day
September 10 . . . . Ganesh Chaturthi
September 22 . . . . Autumnal Equinox
October 31 . . . . Samhain Eve
November 1 . . . . Hallowmas
November 16 . . . . Hecate Night
December 16 . . . . Fairy Queen Eve
December 17 . . . . Saturnalia
December 21 . . . . Winter Solstice
January 9 . . . . Feast of Janus
February 1 . . . . Chinese New Year
February 1 . . . . Oimelc Eve
February 2 . . . . Candlemas
February 15 . . . . Lupercalia
March 1 . . . . Matronalia
March 19 . . . . Minerva's Day

Art Director . . . . Gwion Vran

Astrologer . . . . Dikki-Jo Mullen

Climatologist . . . . Tom C. Lang

Cover Art and Design. . . . Kathryn Sky-Peck

Sales . . . . Ellen Lynch

Bookkeeping . . . . D. Lamoureux

Fulfillment . . . . Casey M.

ANDREW THEITIC
Executive Editor

JEAN MARIE WALSH
Associate Editor

MAB BORDEN
Copy Editor

❧ CONTENTS ❧

ᘄ Contents ᘄ

Hear golden Titan, whose eternal eye with broad
    survey, illumines all the sky.
Self-born, unwearied in diffusing light, and to all
    eyes the mirrour of delight:
Lord of the seaśons, with thy fiery car and leaping
    coursers, beaming light from far:
With thy right hand the source of morning light, and
    with thy left the father of the night.
Agile and vig'rous, venerable Sun, fiery and bright
    around the heav'ns you run.
Foe to the wicked, but the good man's guide, o'er all
    his steps propitious you preside:
With various founding, golden lyre, 'tis mine to fill
    the world with harmony divine.
Father of ages, guide of prosp'rous deeds, the
    world's commander, borne by lucid steeds,
Immortal Jove, all-searching, bearing light, source of
    existence, pure and fiery bright
Bearer of fruit, almighty lord of years, agil and
    warm, whom ev'ry pow'r reveres.
Great eye of Nature and the starry skies, doom'd
    with immortal flames to set and rise
Dispensing justice, lover of the stream, the world's
    great despot, and o'er all supreme.
Faithful defender, and the eye of right, of steeds the
    ruler, and of life the light:
With founding whip four fiery steeds you guide,
    when in the car of day you glorious ride.
Propitious on these mystic labours shine, and bless
    thy suppliants with a life divine.

ORPHIC HYMN TO THE SUN

Yesterday, Today and Tomorrow

by Timi Chasen

MATTERS OF THE GRAVE The mourning of a loved one can take a variety of forms, being colored by culture and the time period in which the decedent passed. What does not change is the need of the survivors to find peace, as well as acceptance of their loss and a return to everyday life. In the highly structured society of Victorian England, mourning practices matched the complexity of the culture. Typically, on the death of a family member, the household members would meticulously cover all mirrors and all family portraits, believing that the spirits of the deceased could inhabit mirrors and photos, enticing the living to join them in their new state. The women of the home would also make sure to tie the front doorknob with a black silk cloth so that all who entered knew to speak in hushed tones.

Among the most peculiar customs were funeral dolls and mourning kits. In a time when infant mortality was high, it was not uncommon for the family to commission the making of a grave doll. This life sized wax doll was made in the likeness of the dead child. In fact, the image would be dressed in clothing from the wardrobe of the dearly departed. In some instances, the doll would stay in the home after the burial of the body, placed in a crib or in a prominent spot.

NOT JUST A GARDEN It is human nature to crow about our accomplishments and worth. In modern times this might include an expensive car, fine

jewelery and flashing large amounts of cash. Another sure sign of wealth is a finely built home surrounded by equally fine lawns and gardens with the requisite gnome, fairy or hobgoblin statues adorning the environs. In the not so distant past of the eighteenth century the wealthy lived life on a grander scale. Their homes were often as big as small castles, the surrounding estates expansive with ornate gardens.

Equally important to the wealthy of yesteryear was the desire to display a sense of introspective melancholy, intellectual prowess and spiritual purity to the world around them. Their serene gardens certainly projected the melancholy that the society of the 18th century valued. To demonstrate their commitment to intellect and spirituality the wealthy would erect small rough hewn abodes among the gardens and of course hire a hermit/druid to inhabit the simple dwellings. These hermits for hire were expected to stay on the property for seven years, appearing before visitors in bedraggled clothing, with a proper set of spectacles and a bible in hand. To the aristocrats' minds, this indeed would project a life of purity, albeit one sheltered from true hardships.

DANCE OF THE WILD MEN
Every five years, deep in the Alps in the most southern region of Bavaria, the town of Oberstdorf sees the Old Ones come to life in the guise of the

Wilde Mändle Tanz, the dance of the wild men. This dance, consisting of 13 men, is dedicated to the Germanic God Donar (Thor) and has been celebrated for several centuries. The men who make up this wild band of dancers are recruited from local families that have been living in the area for centuries. The men are clad from head to toe in moss, lichens and fir, each man tasked with fabricating his own costume.

The performance begins with the leader blowing a bull's horn, asking the band of dancers, "Will the wild men follow the call and hurry forward?" The rhythmic music propels the band into an athletic dance, increasing in complexity of gymnastics and required control. The wild men end their performance with a ritual song and a toast of mead.

The dance celebrates an occasion when Donar saved the town. In 1648 after the plague had killed 800 villagers, it only ended after some brave men danced through the town disguised as wild men. Since that time the town has not missed an opportunity to celebrate their connection to Donar through reenactment of this sacred dance.

BUNNY BUNNY On the first of any given month, even before getting out of bed, you might hear many utter, "Rabbit rabbit," "Bunny bunny," "White Rabbit" or some other refrain addressed to our cotton tailed friends. All this is done to ensure a good month to come as we verbally rub the proverbial rabbit's foot. Once the solemn ritual has been executed, then and only then, is it proper to make like a bunny and hop into the surely favorable month to come.

The origin of this practice is shrouded in the annals of the past. The first instance record was in *Notes and Queries* where an author of an article related "My two daughters are in the

habit of saying 'Rabbits!' on the first day of each month. The word must be spoken aloud, and be the first word said in the month. It brings luck for that month. Other children, I find, use the same formula." This custom has a long history in England, as well as New England. Needless to say, bunnies have been known as the carriers of all sorts of luck throughout history.

BIG BANG Recently, scientists have been paying a good deal of attention to Betelgeuse, a reddish star in the constellation of Orion. While it is one of the brightest objects in the sky, scientists have detected a dimming of the light from this star. Does this fading tell of dramatic action to take place or is it just a strange phenomenon of stellar physics?

Some scientists have suggested that the fading light of Betelgeuse is indeed a portent of a dramatic event to come—it may be entering a pre-supernova stage, where a star begins to dim just before a dramatic collapse that preceeds a fierce explosion.

Betelgeuse is classified as a red giant star, which is just 642.5 light years away from our own star, the Sun. A supernova of this star would be the closest to earth that such an event has occured in recorded history. Interestingly, the predicted supernova could occur anytime in the next few years, but it would have actually ocurred roughly 600 years prior to its observation from Earth.

When Betelgeuse does go supernova, it will be so bright that viewing stars close to it would be nearly impossible. In fact, it would be by far the single brightest object in the sky save the Moon. All being said and done, this dimming of Betelgeuse could quite simply be a phenomenon of magnetic fields creating a visual anamoly. The only way to know for sure is to simply observe.

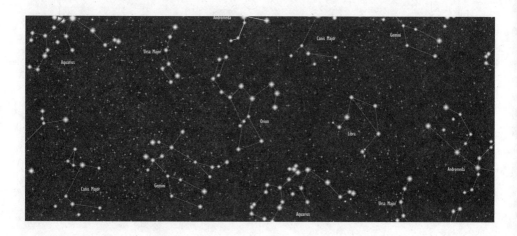

www.TheWitchesAlmanac.com

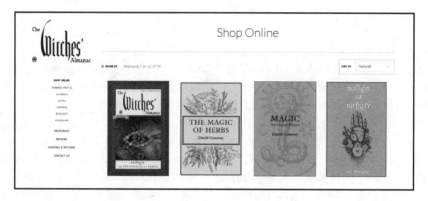

Shop Online

Author Bios

Meet New Contributors

Phoenix	Penny Cabot
Gwion Raven	Seamus Black
Nerites	Josephine McCarthy
Janean Strong	Misha Magdalene
Malorie Vaudoise	Richard Levy

Merry Meetings

A candle in the window, a fire on the hearth,
a discourse over tea...

Come Meet Raymond Buckland

Come visit us at the Witches' Almanac website

News from The Witches' Almanac

Glad tidings from the staff

GOING TO PRESS with *The Witches' Almanac*. This year is even more exciting. The Witches' Almanac as a publishing enterprise has completed 50 years of serving our community!

Pouring over all the tomes we have published, we realized that ours has been a voice for the collective community. The authors who have graced the pages of *The Witches' Almanac* include the likes of Elizabeth Pepper, Leo Martello, Hans Holzer, Ray Buckland, Robert Anton Wilson, Sybil Leek, Theodore Mills, Michael Howard, Gwen Thompson and Charles Leland, to name some that have passed. Recently we have been blessed with fine articles by David Conway, Paul Huson, Dolores Ashcroft-Nowicki, Maxine Sanders, Selena Fox and Judika Illes.

In taking stock of the last 50 years, we thought there could be no better way to honor the past than to create an Anniversary Edition—an anthology of half a century of collected magical lore. We have included more than 200 articles that represent the best of the best.

Also, we are pleased to announce the printing of Harry M. Hyatt's seminal work *Hoodoo—Conjuration—Witchcraft—Rootwork*. Hyatt's masterwork was first published in five thick volumes during 1970–78 and has long been nearly impossible to obtain. Our 13-volume set includes all five volumes as well as attendant works by Michael Bell. This set is a must have for Hoodoo and Conjure workers.

As was the case last year, there are two editions of *The Witches' Almanac*. Our Classic Edition, offered at TheWitchesAlmanac.com and at select shops, is our full book. The Standard Edition is the abridged version offered through Amazon.

The 2021 *Witches' Almanac Wall Calendar* will delight the tree lover: this year's calendar theme is the trees of *Celtic Tree Magic*.

As time marches on, we invariably say goodbye or welcome to staff members. This year, our copy editor Anthony Teth is journeying onward. We wish him the best as he moves forward in his life. We are pleased to welcome Mab Borden as our new copy editor. She brings a breadth of academic experience, and is surviving through the busyness of her first issue.

We have often been asked if we could produce a pendant of *The Witches' Almanac's* logo. We are very happy to report that we now have our logo, desinged by Elizabeth Pepper, available in sterling silver. See our ad at the back of this Almanac for details.

Finally, this year we are proud to offer you the option of paying for your online order by using Bitcoin crypto currency!

Wand Making:
THE FORAGE OF SACRED ROWAN

ROWAN, *fid na ndrud* (the Druid's tree) in Gaelic and also known as the mountain ash, is a tree steeped in Celtic folklore. Rowan got its name from the Norse word *runa* (charm) and in lore is the tree from which the first woman was made, and also that which saved the god Thor from drowning. According to Elizabeth Pepper, rowan is a Scottish word, derived from the Gaelic *rudha-an* (the red one). Its Celtic connection to the Ogham is the letter *L for Luis* (flame or radiance), and its symbolic meaning is protection, psychic communication, divination, healing and connection with the Spirit World.

Rowan is known for its energy for creativity and clarity and as the tree of life in Celtic mythology. Rowan reminds Witches to keep their emotions under control for their own wellbeing and protection. It also guards from outside energies, spells and enchantments and allows for greater discrimination between common sense and superstition. Its energies invoke all deities, assist in calling for the spirits, guides and elementals, and enhance our creativity.

The rowan tree has been guarded by many things: giants, bulls and 24 yellow cats, just to name a few. The giant takes his herd of goats to graze, leaving the rowan unattended from time to time. The bull wanders off to graze and nap, doing the same. The 24 yellow cats, however, perch nicely in the trees and wander round its base, never leaving the rowan unattended.

In *The King of Ireland's Son*, Padraic Colum tells a story about a red herb placed around the cats' necks so that the rowan berries could be taken.

> *"Morag gave grains to the Little Red Hen and begged for words. After a while the Little Red Hen murmured, 'There are things I know, and things I don't know, but I do know what grows near the ground, and if you pull a certain herb, and put it round the necks of the cats, they will not be able to see in the light nor in the dark. And tomorrow is the day of Sowain.'"*

> *[Colum 1921: 278]*

This is supposedly how the berries were taken.

The Banshee and the Pooka are Fae that rule the tree around Sowain—

or Samhain—from late October to November 2, when the veil between the worlds is at its thinnest. This is the only time you may not forage from a rowan tree, for if you should do so, you forage at your own risk, as both Banshees and Pooka are wild and can be disruptive.

Do not take or cut the rowan branch from the tree before making a request and offering to the Faerie King of Munster. He must accept your gift before you may touch the branch. Tread lightly with the Fae folk, and when asking anything from their forests, bow with gifts and with gratitude. On the New Moon, find the rowan tree you wish to ask for a wand branch. Place a piece of parchment with your Witch name on it under the tree. As an offering, fill a red satin bag with red clover blossoms, three drops of red wine, catnip and three drops of milk.

Go back to the tree of choice on the Full Moon. If the Faerie King has taken your parchment, and only if the parchment is gone, you may place the offering at the base of the rowan tree. Wait three days and three nights to return. If he has taken your satchel, he has received your gifts and requests and you may now take a fallen branch or twig from this tree. Remember to take only one branch for each request.

Place the branch on an altar and cast a circle. Draw in the energy of Aine, the daughter of Manannán mac Lir who is Lord of the Sea. Ask Aine to bless this wood for magical workings and state, "it is fixed."

Leave the bark intact because it is the flesh of the Fae. Amethyst, clear quartz, carnelian, bloodstone and red jasper have a harmonious energy with the rowan. Metals are not a favorite of the Fae-folk,

so it is not recommended that you use metal wires or bindings to secure your stones. Once the wand is complete, on the New Moon with an aspect in Leo cast a circle to charge and fix the wand. Hold the wood with both hands and say:

I draw into the center of this circle the presence of Aine and the Faerie King of Munster.

I ask for your blessing on this wood, Aine.

I ask for your blessing on this wood, great Faerie King.

I ask that this wand be charged with the correct and harmonious energies and forces of the universe and for the good of all.

I charge this wand to do my bidding.

I fix this wand to my energy so that it answers to no other.

It is fixed!

—PENNY CABOT

DINNER WITH THE GODS

IMAGINE you received a phone call from your favorite deity. It just so happens they'll be in town this weekend and they want to come to your house for dinner. How would you go about welcoming them into your home, providing them food and entertaining them?

Many Pagan and Witchcraft practices center around invoking, evoking and inviting the Gods to magical rites. Occasionally they show up—many times they don't. How can you increase the likelihood that the Gods will make it to your ritual? Well, you can start by creating a meal they can't resist.

In virtually every culture, past and present, the Gods have received offerings. Food is one of the most common offerings. Read through most mythologies and histories and you'll find all sorts of food offerings made to the Gods. Most importantly, this practice still works today. The basic steps are described below.

Send an invite. If you want someone to show up for a party, the first step is to invite them. You tell your anticipated guests what day the celebration is, what time of day it starts, and why you're having this get together in the first place. It's the same when inviting the Gods to dine with you. So often, the Gods are invited to the party after the party has started. Don't wait for your ritual

dinner to start before asking them to attend! Literally write out a request for the god of your choice to attend your event. Put the invitation on an altar dedicated to them or underneath their statue or write it on the back of a picture you've printed of them.

Clean the temple. There's a good chance that before you invite friends and family over for a weekend barbecue or birthday celebration, you tidy your house. Maybe you mow the lawn, vacuum the living room and make sure there's a new roll of toilet paper in the bathroom. It's the same when the Gods come to dinner. Give your temple space a quick spruce up. You can put fresh flowers on the altar, dust the shelves in your ritual room and clear away the bills and homework from the kitchen table where you're planning to put your offerings.

Fill the table with their favorite things. If you were throwing a birthday party, you might decorate the table with a festive tablecloth, balloons, streamers and gifts. What would your Gods appreciate at their special dinner? Think about which items you associate with them. For example, keys, ruby red grapes, garlands of ivy or cedar, bowls filled with pomegranate seeds, cigars and rum all have associations with particular deities. The more the Gods recognize the space you are creating for this meal, the more likely they are to stop by.

Cook food the Gods will recognize. If you invited your best friend over to dinner, what would you make for them? Perhaps you'd make their favorite pasta dish with fresh vegetables and serve that

bottle of wine they love so much. Do exactly that for the Gods you want at your ritual. Do a little research on your Gods, where they came from, when they were most prominently worshipped and which foods were routinely served at their celebrations and rituals. In ancient Sumer, for example, the devotees of Inanna would give her dates, honey and meats spiced with cumin, coriander, garlic, and onion. Make those same offerings today. Inanna would recognize those dishes and be more likely to show up to your rites.

People like to spend time with others who are like minded, who make them laugh and feel welcome when they spend time with them. It's exactly the same with the Gods. Invite them over, make them feel welcome and feed them the food and drink they love.

−GWION RAVEN

Lady of the Rainbow

The true harvest of my life is intangible— a little star dust caught, a portion of the rainbow I have clutched...

–Henry David Thoreau

WHO WOULDN'T WANT a fairy godparent with all-seeing eyes? When asked, she protects you. She leads you to succeed. She is your companion in finding harmony and when your life is done, she is your final guide.

Iris' name, meaning rainbow, also means the iris flower, the iris of an eye and the florescent, eye-like ocelli on a peacock's tail. Her Roman counterpart is Arcus. She is the great eye of heaven— we only see the upper half of her iris as the lower half peers into the underworld.

Though few myths about Iris have survived, perhaps they once existed, considering that she is older than the Greek language. Maybe her name was replaced through misplaced epithets or she changed status in the Greek pantheon. Like a rainbow, her mythology is nebulous.

Iris travels between destinations via rainbow, although she was probably originally the rainbow itself. Golden winged, Iris carries a herald's caduceus and a pitcher. She is often portrayed with a rainbow corona about her head.

Plutarch recorded that, Iris, "has the head of a bull and consumes the water of streams." Eastern European tradition also shows the rainbow as a serpent gulping water, and in Estonia it has an ox's head. The rainbow is considered androgynous—some cultures believe passing under a rainbow will change a person's gender. Even the I Ching counsels that the rainbow is a combination of yin and yang.

The Proto-Indo-Europeans

Iris is derived either from the Indo-

European word *wei*, meaning to bend, as in pulling back a bow, or from *rei* meaning striped. The word iris exists in 19 different languages. The thunder God's rainbow is also found in many cultures. For example, the Hindu heavenly archer Indra uses it to slay a primordial serpent. The Goddess Iris was associated with the thunder God Zeus in a Proto-Indo-European pantheon long before coming to Greece.

Zeus' Slavic counterpart Perun uses a stylized iris symbol. The Slavs call the blue iris *perunika*, which means Perun thunder flower. It is believed to grow where lightning has struck and protects against thunderstrikes. Perun's consort is Perunika or Mokosh (Great Mother). *Mokosh* derives from the Proto-Indo-European word for wet. Archaeological evidence for Mokosh goes back to the 7th Century B.C.E. when she was a Goddess of fertility and death.

The Greeks

Iris' epithets include golden winged, swift footed, wind-swift footed, dewy, storm swift, balanced, glory of the sky, cloud borne and sister of the winds. She is descended from the Greek Gods of sea, sky and Earth. She was born of Electra, a sea nymph and cloud nymph, and Thaumas, a God of the ocean who was the child of Earth and sea. Her father's name means wonder and is the root word for thaumaturgy. Called the daughter of wonder, Iris must have inherited his magic.

The only recorded worship of Iris was that the Delians gave her offerings of honey, wheat and dried fig cakes. Iris might be an aspect of Hekate, who was also frequently worshipped in the islands around Delos. Both Goddesses are golden winged, older than the Greek pantheon, served as Hera's handmaidens and are associated with the *drakontes* (dragons.)

Iris' functions

When Iris delivers messages, she often shapeshifts into someone the recipient knows. In the oldest myths, she was Zeus' messenger. Over time, however, Hermes replaced her and Iris became loyal to Hera. As a cup bearer Iris is highly trusted and has aided both man and God. She goes where many other Gods cannot. Because Greek women would never hold this role, this is one of her anomalies.

Using her pitcher she gathers sea water to refill clouds with rain. Undoubtedly Iris was once revered for her role in quickening the seeds of newly planted fields. In her role as witness to oaths, she gathers water from the Styx.

A God that drinks it and tells a lie will be comatose for a year then banned from Olympus for nine more.

After marrying Zephyr, the west wind, Iris bore Pothos, one of the three Erotes, winged gods of desire whose arrows inspire love and lust. You are likely familiar with Cupid, the Roman counterpart of Eros, another of the Erotes. In this sense, Iris is literally the mother of love. Although she doesn't start quarrels, Iris spreads her share of discord on behalf of her sponsors, but even then she attempts to solve disputes first.

She is very similar to the original conception of her sisters the Harpies— beautiful, winged women. Only over time did they become depicted as ugly with vultures' bodies. Homer said Iris' surname is Aellopos, a reference to the harpy Aello. Since that name means storm swift, she may actually be Iris! If so, Aello was known for capturing people on their way to Tartarus and torturing them. Several accounts exist of Iris' duties as a psychopomp—she was asked to sever the souls of both Hercules and Dido. Though Iris is said to be sweet tempered with no enemies, clearly she should be treated respectfully.

Planting irises on graves is a global tradition, and some say Iris specifically guides women. In Turkey, however, irises are also planted on soldiers' graves .

The flower in this myth is not today's hyacinth. One case can be made that larkspur has "AI" on its blossom. Traditionally, though, the hyacinth is thought to be an iris. Iris' noted gender ambiguity adds a twist here, as Hyacinthus could be yet another aspect of Iris. At Hyacinthus' tomb, on which Iris is also depicted, he is uncharacteristically portrayed with facial hair—and some species of iris blossoms have the distinction of being bearded!

The iris flower is apotropaic—it wards against the evil eye. When used as a magical ingredient the iris corm is called orris root. It is used in spells for love, protection, purification, wisdom, nobility, faith, balance, communication, courage, victory and as a sacred oil.

The peacock

Iris' sacred animal, the peacock, is an excellent guardian. It has been called the world's most aggressive bird and its greatest enemy is the snake. To Greeks and Romans peacock feathers were all-seeing talismans against the evil eye. They were thought to transform snake venom into solar iridescence. Pliny recorded that magicians took amethysts inscribed with the Sun and Moon and hung them about their necks with peacock hairs and swallow feathers for protection against sorcery. Peacocks commonly decorated Greek and Roman women's funerary art to symbolize resurrection and immortality because it was believed that peacocks' bodies did not decay.

The peacock is also sacred to Hera in the same manner that Iris, as Hera's handmaiden, belongs to her. While Hera's bird was originally the cuckoo, the peacock entered Greek awareness on Samos where the golden peacock was introduced. After Athenians sacked the island in 440 B.C.E., it became the site of Hera's largest temple. Like Iris, these peacocks had golden wings—one can't help but wonder who this flock was dedicated to before Hera.

The Temperance card

The figure on the Temperance tarot card has alternately been recognized as the Archangel Michael or Iris. The field of blooming irises is the most obvious indication it is Iris. She stands in a liminal place, neither on shore nor in the water and in older decks a rainbow arcs behind her. It symbolizes Iris' ability to access all realms.

On the card, Iris is repeatedly mixing the golden vessel of consciousness into the silver vessel of unconsciousness. In Jungian terms the Temperance card represents integrating the self through the balance and exchange of opposites. Through tempering the other two parts of Plato's tripartite soul, appetite

and logic, harmony is achieved. Commonly, Temperance bears a sun or its alchemical symbol which represents the earthly connection with the divine. A.E. Waite said, "It is called Temperance fantastically, because, when the rule of it obtains in our consciousness, it tempers, combines and harmonises (sic) the psychic and material natures…" that it is "the analogy of solar light, realized in the third part of our human triplicity."

Over time Temperance has come to mean moderation, but that wasn't always so. Originally, Temperance was not about avoiding the extremes, but integrating them. Tempering takes patience, timing and balance. Without these qualities, the process cannot succeed. Temperance is androgynous, sometimes female and sometimes male. According to Elemire Zolla, "(the androgyne's) peculiar symbolic character consists in a blend of androgyny with a conjunction of the human and the divine."

In the tarot, Temperance lies between Death and Judgment, a reminder that that humans don't always achieve well balanced harmony on the first try. Only through slow, thorough repetition can we achieve singularity. This is the card of reincarnation—its work is rarely done in one lifetime.

Ever watchful, Iris is more than a messenger. She persuades us to act and she is here to guide us through. She represents what is truly noble— achieving balance, tempering our hungers, finding harmony in our logic and shooting for the divine.

—NIALLA

A Symbol of Times Past

A word from the editor:

I recently heard an online interview of David Rankine hosted by Julian Vayne on a YouTube channel called My Magical Thing. *The show is an ongoing series of interviews with occult practitioners, asking them to show and tell about a prized magical object that they own. David Rankine was kind enough to follow up on the interview by giving The Witches' Almanac a bit more of a personal look into his magical thing—a lamen made by Samuel Lidell MacGregor Mathers.*

—Andrew Theitic

The gift

ON MY 40th BIRTHDAY I received a unique birthday present from occult legend, Stephen Skinner. When we had met in 2004, we just clicked, and within five minutes we had decided to found Golden Hoard Press and collaborate together on making rare grimoire texts available in the Sourceworks of Ceremonial Magic series. On my birthday a year later, Stephen presented me with a gift that left me stunned.

As grimoire magicians we are both always keen to know the provenance of magical texts, items, etc., so Stephen explained that the lamen he presented me had been made by Samuel Lidell MacGregor Mathers. He was one of the cofounders of the Hermetic Order of the Golden Dawn in 1888 and one of the most significant figures in the Victorian occult revival. I knew that almost all of Mather's paraphernalia had been destroyed after his death by his wife Moina Mathers. This makes the lamen incredibly special, having been owned by Mathers and also made by his own hand.

In the 1920s Moina befriended a young occult artist who would later become known for her esoteric art, Ithell Colquhoun. It was to her that Moina gave the lamen I now own. Ithell Colquhuon passed the lamen on to the occult author Francis X. King, who would collaborate with Stephen on several books before his death in 1994. Francis gave Stephen the lamen, and from his hands it was gifted to me.

Symbols and their meanings

The lamen's symbols are clearly based on those used by the Golden Dawn, but with changes. The symbol of the Golden Dawn is a cross on top of an upward pointing equilateral triangle with a rising sun and its rays inside. The triangle with the rising sun represents the outer order, the Hermetic Order of the Golden Dawn. The internal sun represents the solar sephira of Tiphereth on the Qabalistic Tree of Life, which symbolizes the achievement of magical proficiency.

Although based on the Golden Dawn imagery, the symbol on the lamen clearly differs from it by positioning the cross inside the triangle. As this places the symbol of the inner order within that of the outer order, it is possible that Mathers did this to emphasize his perception of himself as the head of the Golden Dawn. Despite the conflicts of 1900 and the schisms that followed, Mathers is likely to have considered himself the order's true head and the symbols he chose for this lamen may reflect this position.

The cross with a rose in its center represents the inner order of the Golden Dawn, the Rosae Rubae et Aurae Crucis, or Ruby Rose and Golden Cross. It can also represent the Supernal Triad, the uppermost Sephirot of the Qabalistic Tree of Life: Kether, Chokmah and Binah. The lamen places a spiral rather than a rose at the center of the cross. This may have been a stylistic choice as it might simply be easier than making a rose, or Mathers may have decided a spiral was more appropriate for his lamen. Positioning a spiral in the center of the cross could symbolize the connection of the human to the divine, and the journey to realization of the divine within the self. This might also represent Mathers' view of himself as the link to the Secret Chiefs, the spirit beings who allegedly provided the impetus for the creation of the order and the spiritual authority to run it.

These are speculations and we may never know for sure, but one thing that is certain is that it is a wonderful piece of magical history, and I am honoured and delighted to have ended up as its custodian.

—DAVID RANKINE

For more information about the lamen and the history of this unique item, Mr. Rankine's My Magical Thing *interview can be found at https://www.youtube.com/watch?v=F_xLCQVnh-U.*

Baba Yaga, The Wild Witch of the Woods

IMAGINE that you are lost in a deep, dark, ancient forest. You knew better than to wander off the well-worn path, but you couldn't help yourself. The trees are thick, creating a canopy of darkness above you, blocking out even the Sun. From above the branches you hear a crack and a cackle. You don't let that stop you, but rather push ahead, coming to a clearing in the trees. You rub your eyes in disbelief. In the center of the clearing is a ring of fence, with each post topped by a flaming skull. Within the ring, scratching its way around the center is a little hut walking around on chicken legs. Lights are shining from its windows as if its eyes were open.

You have reached the hut of Baba Yaga, and there is no turning back.

Her origins

In Slavic and Russian folk tales there is an old woman who lives in a hut deep in the woods. However, she is not the type of creature you want to encounter while lost because she is just as likely to eat you as help you. She is Baba Yaga and her stories have been told for longer than written record and they remain a vital part of eastern European and Russian culture to this day.

Her origins are obscure, but she is included in many Slavic folk tales. Baba Yaga is featured both as the lone Witch in the woods and also as part of a trio of sisters or cousins. In some stories she is killed only to be resurrected or show up again in the next story. In these tales, her name seems to be a title whose owner changes over time.

Her appearance

The appearance of Baba Yaga across her stories is fairly consistent. She is always seen as an old hag with a long hooked nose and a long hooked chin. She is thin, tall and scrawny. Her epithet of "bony leg" in some tales wasn't just in reference to her being thin, but having one leg made only of bone, missing its flesh. In many folk stories when someone enters her hut, she takes up the entirety of the space with her long limbs stretching from one end of the house to the other.

What makes her descriptions so interesting is the fact that the other characters are rarely described in detail, but a lot of emphasis is placed on how ugly, old and scary Baba Yaga appears. It's possible that the focus on her aging body may connect to the fact that she is a ruler over death itself.

Baba Yaga's teeth are also a point of detailed focus. They are long and pointed or made from metal. She is seen using a file to sharpen her teeth, often when her potential victim is in the other room attempting to complete the impossible tasks that she has assigned to them.

Her connection to Fire

Baba Yaga's hut is hemmed in by a fence made of flaming skulls. This shows again her relationship to life and death, because the skulls potentially belong to those who got lost in the woods and were unable to complete her tasks. However, this is also a sign of her connection to Fire.

For those that live in the cold climates of the North, Fire is life. It means more than cooking or having something pretty to stare into—fire keeps you alive.

In many of the folk tales, Baba Yaga is set alightor shoved into a stove by those that are trying to escape her wrath. Although she is killed in these stories, she does not die. Much like the phoenix, the Fire bird of Russian myth, she rises again or returns. Fire doesn't kill her, but rather promotes her regeneration.

Her allies

Baba Yaga may be a Witch living alone in the woods, but she isn't actually alone. There are many helpers in her hut and the surrounding woods, both seen and unseen. In some tales the helpers don't help her at all, but help her hostages to escape. These allies come in many forms, including a black cat; a rat; mice; a frog; a firebird; disembodied hands; three riders that represent the dawn, the day and the night; mushrooms; birds; eagles; and more. She is able to talk to the plants and animals, getting them to do her bidding which is why she is seen as a Goddess of Earth.

Your own free will

Baba Yaga may represent an older spirit or Goddess of initiation. Much of her symbolism and the repetitive patterns in her folk tales lend credence to her being an initiatrix. One of these signs is her question to those who come to her seeking help or guidance: "Do you come here of

your own free will?" Baba Yaga asks this question to those in her clutches.

Working with her now

How do modern Witchcraft practitioners work with this wild spirit of the dark woods? How does someone approach such a Goddess when the response might be getting devoured? Baba Yaga is a demanding Goddess. She doesn't suffer fools and has high expectations. If you are called to work with Baba Yaga it's important that you know what you're getting yourself into. She is demanding and will ask you to complete tasks that seem impossible, but if you honor her wishes and stick with it, your rewards will be greater than you could imagine.

If you are interested in opening up a relationship with this Goddess here are some ways to get started:

- **Read**. Immerse yourself in Russian and Slavic folk tales. There is a lot of information on how to best connect with Baba Yaga in these stories.

- **Make space**. Create an altar, no matter how big or small, for Baba Yaga in your home. Place items on it that connect to her energy.

- **Make offerings**. This can take the form of vodka, food, incense or singing.

- **Sort**. Baba Yaga often requires those that stumble into her hut to sort, items such as wheat from chaff or poppy seeds and grains of dirt. Baba Yaga may ask you to sort out your life, your home or your belongings.

Baba Yaga has been an important character in Russia and eastern Europe for hundreds, if not, thousands of years. Awareness of her on a larger scale has grown in recent years. She is not only a Goddess of the forest and Earth, but a Goddess of life and death. She can help you through the most difficult and challenging moments in life and find your own power to make it through. She won't be soft and tender about it, but she will help you get the work done and find your way through the dark night of the soul to a stronger you.

—PHOENIX

THE WAY OF THE SUN

"That the sun moves in a particular course must have been one of the first observations which primitive man made in regard to the movements of celestial bodies."

–William Wells Newell, Founder of the American Folklore Society

WE TAKE IT FOR GRANTED that the Sun will rise every morning, and we limit our thoughts of its effects to photosynthesis and the damage it can cause to our skin. Our ancestors attributed much more to the solar body. Noticing that the Sun traveled from East to West and that things grew and prospered with the Sun, people began to associate the direction in which it moved as beneficial. Performing acts in the direction of the Sun, deosil, was propitious. Going against the direction of the Sun, widdershins, led to failure.

When making sauces, puddings or cakes, cooks stirred in a clockwise direction lest the cooking go wrong. Stirring in the direction of the Sun made good bread, light cakes and fluffy eggs. Even the teapot was stirred clockwise—to stir counterclockwise could stir up a quarrel. Cooks also paid attention to the ascendancy of the Sun, baking a cake in the morning so that it would rise as the Sun ascended. They avoided baking it in the afternoon, fearing that it would sink as the Sun sank. The dinner table was laid in a clockwise direction and wine was also passed thusly, for it was believed that one must never go against the Sun.

Sailors coiled their ropes in the direction of the Sun. When starting a journey, they circled clockwise before heading to their destination. Expectant mothers walked round a church three times in order to ensure a safe and easy delivery. Fire was carried around infants and mothers for protection against faeries. To relieve the pain of rheumatism, sufferers rubbed the affected area sunwise. In the Scottish Highlands, a seer walked rapidly three times deosil around the person whose future was to be foretold, the combination of direction and the magic number three producing a trance that ignited the divinatory powers.

Many religious practices still follow the way of the Sun. Tibetan Buddhists go around their shrines sunwise. The Hindu *pradakshina*, the circumambulation of sacred places, is also made clockwise. Wiccans cast a circle clockwise.

MORVEN WESTFIELD

A Queer Liminality

Exploring and Embracing the Fluid Gender and

Sexuality of Witch-Gods

MODERN iterations of Witchcraft are often noted for adhering to a theological model which deifies both heterosexuality and a binary gender paradigm. From the dyadic Goddess and God of Gerald Gardner's Wicca and related traditions to the Witchmother and Witchfather found in some lines of Traditional Witchcraft, an explicitly heterosexual female–male gender binary is upheld by many as the definitive truth of their magical theologies. Even within Craft lineages such as the Feri tradition of Victor and Cora Anderson, which overtly embraces queerness of both gender and sexuality, some practitioners have wrestled with the cultural pressure to view the Gods through a binary lens, to see the metagendered, all-encompassing Star Goddess and the androgynous Peacock Angel as a gendered dyad little different from that of their Wiccan or Traditional Witch cousins.

Some years ago, Lynna Landstreet pointed to the appealing universality of this theology, writing that that the Wiccan Goddess and God "represent the forces of creation and destruction, birth and death, Eros and Thanatos," which she beautifully summarized in succinct fashion: "Witches worship sex and death." Female and male, creation and destruction, sex and death. It all seems so simple, doesn't it? Within this binary, the complexities of primal existence can be summarized and canonized in a neat, tidy package.

The appeal of this simplicity and tidiness, however, hides a trap.

To be a Witch is to be a liminal being, one who walks into darkness to bring back wisdom. A Witch is one who explores the worlds between the worlds, who finds the numinous in the light and the dark and the spaces between. It should come as no surprise, then, that the Gods they find in those spaces between often embody and exemplify that same queerness, that same liminality.

It's a trivial matter to find modern queer Witches whose personal gnosis supports and validates this divine liminality, but if historical validation is desired, plenty is available for the discerning researcher. Contemplate the androgynous body of Baphomet—supposedly revered by the Knights Templar and certainly much beloved by modern Witches—identified by Eliphas Lévi as the Sabbatic Goat, with full breasts and erect penis. Look also to the queer Greek God Dionysus, raised as a girl child, who descended to the Underworld and rose again, and whose worshippers would cross dress in their devotional ecstasies. Recall the Norse poem *Völuspá hin skamma*, in which the genderqueer trickster God Loki eats the heart of a Witch, then gives birth as a woman to a line of Witches, becoming quite literally the Witchmother.

Looking to more modern lines of practice, meditate on the oft-quoted line from Doreen Valiente's Charge of the Goddess—words attributed to the Wiccan Goddess—"in the dust of whose feet are the hosts of heaven"in which she reminds us that, "all acts of love and pleasure are my rituals." Building on this key piece of liturgy, Wiccan writers like Yvonne Aburrow have built a compelling argument that the Gods of Gardner's Witch cult needn't be bound to binary notions of gender or sexuality. Consider also the words of writers like Gemma Gary, who flatly dismisses the idea that heterosexuality or binary gender hold any relevance to the Witch Gods. *In The Devil's Dozen: Thirteen Craft Rites* of the Old One, Gary explicitly states that the Old One can take the shape of a woman or a man for the purposes of mystical sexual union with an initiate, then goes on to write that, "in sacred transgression of societal 'normality,' same sex couplings are also to be found in the old lore of the Witches' Sabbath."

Witches are liminal beings, and the Gods of the Witches are likewise liminal, in both body and action. Those who live in the liminal spaces of Witchcraft would do well to remember that "simple" and "tidy" are often code for "reductive." When a Witch simplifies their view of reality for convenience's sake, they also narrow their own vision, and in so doing they risk hiding from their own eyes the very powers they seek. Wise is the Witch who instead chooses to see the Witch Gods as they truly are, numinous and multivalent beings—with all their complexity and queer liminality intact.

—MISHA MAGDALENE

♂ ♀ ○ ⚥ ⚨

SIGILS OF SOUND

THERE ARE numerous ways to utilize pitch within individual praxis which range from the simple to the highly intricate. A simple usage may be to instill a plain white candle with a color through intoning the correct pitch. Similarly one could project color onto plain white paper before drawing a sigil, or take a portion of plain black ink and add another color property to it. The options are vast.

For a more involved process, one may use pitch in combination with kameas, or magic squares. These geometric figures are tables that have a Hebrew letter or a number assigned to each square, and are arranged so that each row, column and diagonal will add up to the same number. A traditional method of drawing sigils is to trace a magical word or planetary name according to its corresponding numbers. However, this can be done with sound as well by drawing upon pitches associated with the Hebrew alphabet as found in the tarot correspondences developed by Paul Foster Case.

Sound and color

To produce this table of correspondences between the tarot and colors, musical pitches and the Hebrew aleph-bet, Paul Foster Case drew upon the Marcotone system of Edward Maryon. This system paired individual pitches with a color, to which Case added a Hebrew letter according to the system used by the Golden Dawn. This gave additional insight into the character of the tarot card they were assigned to. It also provided a clear method of musically differentiating the three groups of Hebrew letters: the mother letters, the double letters, and the simple letters.

The three mother letters are assigned the three primary colors of red, yellow and blue and the pitches C, G# and E:

Mother Letters

Letter	Pitch	Color	Color Type	Element
Aleph	E	Yellow	Primary	Air
Mem	G#	Blue	Primary	Water
Shin	C	Red	Primary	Fire

When combined, these pitches form two major third intervals or an augmented fifth. The colors represent the element to which each of the mother letters is assigned.

The seven double letters are given the following colors and pitches.

Double Letters

Letter	Pitch	Color	Color Type	Element
Peh	C	Red	Primary	Mars
Resh	D	Orange	Secondary	Sun
Beth	E	Yellow	Primary	Mercury
Daleth	F#	Green	Secondary	Venus
Gimmel	G#	Blue	Primary	Moon
Kaph	A#	Violet	Secondary	Jupiter
Tau	A	Blue Violet	Tertiary	Saturn

Here, the double letters produce a whole tone scale. The primary colors are given to the planets whose qualities best represent the corresponding element of the mother letter.

Unlike the major triad formed by the mother letters, the whole tone scale of the double letters is harmonically ambiguous, with no apparent tonal center and so no obvious major or minor tonality. It can also be viewed as the major triad of C having a triad formed of two major thirds placed on top of it, D-F# and F#-A#, or the perfect fifth of the mother

Simple Letters

Letter	Pitch	Color	Color Type	Zodiac Sign
Heh	C	Red	Primary	Aries
Vau	C#	Red Orange	Tertiary	Taurus
Zain	D	Orange	Secondary	Gemini
Chet	D#	Orange Yellow	Tertiary	Cancer
Teth	E	Yellow	Primary	Leo
Yod	F	Yellow Green	Tertiary	Virgo
Lamed	F#	Green	Secondary	Libra
Nun	G	Blue Green	Tertiary	Scorpio
Samekh	G#	Blue	Primary	Sagittarius
Ayin	A	Blue Violet	Tertiary	Capricorn
Tzaddi	A#	Violet	Secondary	Aquarius
Qoph	B	Red Violet	Tertiary	Pisces

letters joined with the augmented fifth of the additional colors.

Among the simple letters, tonality has become broken down further into a representation of the twelve tone or chromatic scale favored by composers such as Schoenberg.

From image to melody

The pitches given to the Hebrew letters in these charts may be written into any of the planetary kameas to enable sigils to be drawn which can be easily translated into melodies to use as part of a working. It is important to remember that the resultant melodies will not necessarily sound pleasing if compared to music typical of the western classical tradition because of its lack of a harmonic center or need for western harmony.

The sigil below has been traced upon the kamea of the Sun, pictured

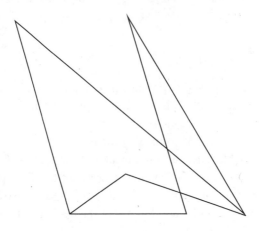

6	32	3	34	35	1
7	11	27	28	8	30
19	14	16	15	23	24
18	20	22	21	17	13
25	29	10	9	26	12
36	5	33	4	2	31

below it, and is designed to promote beauty and growth.

To turn the sigil into a melody, each point of the sigil is translated into its corresponding pitch using the table below.

C	F#/E	G#	F#	F#/C	E
D	E/E	A#/D	A#/D#	D#	F#
F/E	F/F#	F/C#	F/C	A#/G#	A#/F#
F/D#	A#	A#/E	A#/E	F/F	F/G#
A#/C	A#/E	F	E	A#/C#	F/E
F#/C#	C	F#/G#	F#	E	F#/E

The resulting pitches are:

The pitches may be chanted or intoned to equal length notes, to a reduction of the original intention or other key word which is appropriate.

However, the kamea is also able to produce a rhythmic value for each pitch should the practitioner wish. Each note value is calculated by counting the number of squares between one pitch and the next. Hold the first pitch for one quaver beat or eighth note for each square crossed by the line. The final note may be held to either the distance back to the starting note or for a length which is pleasing to the practitioner and suitable to the intent of the sigil.

The initial pitches mentioned above will then generate the following rhythmic values and create the following melody.

If the sigil is to be used as part of a group working, the colors of the flashing tablet associated with the kamea may be used to provide insight into appropriate harmonic intervals useful to create harmonies. A flashing tablet may be created by tracing lines between the numerical values of the kamea in order and then coloring the resulting shapes in one of two complementary colors so no two touching shapes have the same color. When meditated upon the design appears to flash and pulse with energy. Here, the colors violet and yellow would be used to create a flashing tablet. Using either the intervals of an octave and a fourth as given in Newton's *Opticks*, published in 1704, or the pitches associated with those colors, A# and E, would be appropriate.

Below the melody is shown with the inclusion of a drone E producing the octave interval at the start and maintained throughout. It would be equally as effective to sing the melody in octaves.

The octave at which these melodies are sung or chanted is dependent on the capabilities and vocal range of the individual practitioner.

—JERA

Pegasus and his rider
Arthur Rakham

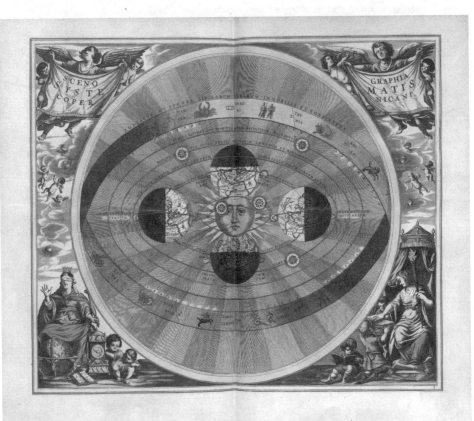

The Solar System
Heliocentric Astrology

EARTH, along with the other planets, revolves around the Sun. In astrology's lengthy history, which stretches back to the dawn of recorded time, this fact is relatively recent news.

The heliocentric, that is the Sun centered universe, was discovered by Nicholas Copernicus, who lived from 1473–1543 C.E. Copernicus was a Polish-German physician, astrologer and mathematician who is remembered as the father of modern astronomy.

Previously the geocentric, that is the Earth centered view of the universe, was accepted as the truth about the cosmos. The geocentric was described by Claudius Ptolemy and had the Sun and stars revolving around planet Earth. Ptolemy was an Egyptian-Greek mathematician, astronomer and astrologer who lived from 100–170 C.E. He drew upon much earlier Babylonian observations to determine how the celestial patterns in the heavens above correlated with the patterns of life and destiny on Earth below.

Most modern astrologers continue to calculate horoscopes like Ptolemy, from the perspective of Earth. Horoscope charts still continue to place Earth at the center of the universe because people who follow astrology seriously agree that the Ptolemaic universe works.

Despite being bombarded by critics and naysayers with the obvious fact that Copernicus accurately described the heliocentric over 500 years ago, astrology continues to follow the earlier model. Planets, such as Uranus, Neptune, Pluto and Chiron, and other celestial bodies, such as the asteroids, which were discovered in modern times are included in the ephemeris tables used by astrologers just as if they too are orbiting Earth. Why? The reason is simple: Ptolemy's geocentric Earth centered universe works for us because we live on planet Earth. From the earthly perspective the magnetic energies traveling toward the planet through outer space do impact Earth as if it is the center of the universe.

Most astrologers would agree that for the purpose of horoscope calculation Copernicus' heliocentric universe would only be valid if somehow it would be possible to reside on the Sun. In fact, the astrologers of the future will probably have to develop separate zodiac systems. Eventually, if Mars and other planets are colonized the dome of the surrounding space will have corresponding energy variances, and Earth centered horoscopes probably won't work.

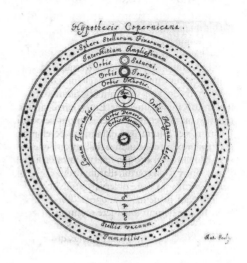

There are exceptions, however. There are a few recent astrologers who do prefer to use charts calculated using the heliocentric ephemeris. Benjamin Franklin, often praised as the greatest astrologer who ever lived, made references to using heliocentric astrology, although he followed the more familiar geocentric astrology in calculating his almanacs. Some contemporary astrologers emulate Dr. Franklin and actually consult both types of charts. One heliocentric astrologer who does this type of dual analysis calls it a twofold Gemini-like practice, alluding to the twins.

Those who would like to experiment with Sun-centered astrology will find that this kind of horoscope is quite different in several ways:

- There is no retrograde motion. Even though it is very influential, retrograde motion is an optical illusion viewed from the perspective of Earth.
- The placements of Mercury, Venus

and Mars are radically different.

- The planets from Jupiter out also have different placements, but they will vary less than the inner planets .
- There are no nodes of the Moon. Instead planetary nodes might be included.
- There are no Sun or Moon placements.
- Earth will be added instead of the Sun. The Earth sign opposes the familiar Sun sign. They are placed 180 degrees apart, exactly across the zodiac.

Some astrologers use the familiar house placements and zodiac in heliocentric astrology. Other practitioners use a plain circular wheel with only the planetary placements, but this creates a very blank and empty looking diagram.

A good way to take a look at heliocentric astrology is to start with considering the Earth sign. Determine whether what it indicates seems to hold true. If so, then further studies can be easily pursued. Here are some keywords to offer a quick glance at how the Earth sign, the single most significant factor in a heliocentric horoscope, might be interpreted. The sun sign in the geocentric chart is listed in bold with the description of the corresponding Earth sign in the heliocentric chart .

- **Aries** Your Earth sign is Libra. You seek a shield from the harshness of life, always looking for better options.
- **Taurus** Your Earth sign is Scorpio.

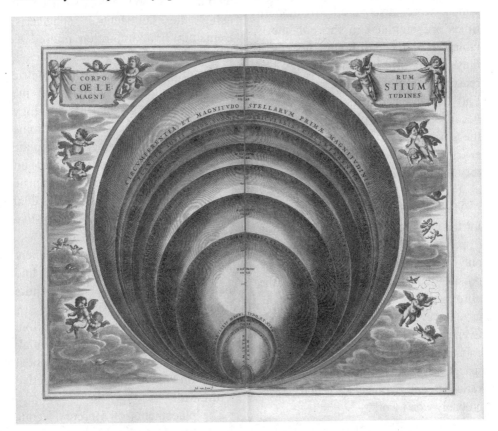

Secretive, grounded and possessive, your strong opinions invite controversy.

- **Gemini** Your Earth sign is Sagittarius. Planning where to go and what to do next, the dynamics of change exhilarate you.
- **Cancer** Your Earth sign is Capricorn. Serious and reserved, you value reliability. Highly motivated, you are a catalyst.
- **Leo** Your Earth Sign is Aquarius. Friendly and group oriented, you like to consider broad perspectives and wider viewpoints.
- **Virgo** Your Earth sign is Pisces. Fanciful and creative, you seek beauty. Charitable, you empathize with those in need.
- **Libra** Your Earth sign is Aries. An eternal rebel, you act quickly when faced with a challenge.
- **Scorpio** Your Earth sign is Taurus. Possessive and systematic, you prefer to develop proficiency in all you attempt.
- **Sagittarius** Your Earth sign is Gemini. Curious and fluid, to avoid being trapped you leave an exit open, a way out.
- **Capricorn** Your Earth sign is Cancer. Vulnerable and sensitive, you are attached to traditions and memories.
- **Aquarius** Your Earth Sign is Leo. Authoritative and dignified, you are critical of the ordinary and inferior.
- **Pisces** Your Earth Sign is Virgo. You analyze concerns and challenges, correcting and organizing priorities.

Please see this year's Celebrity Horoscope featuring Dion Fortune. Read her biography and then compare it to the heliocentric version of her natal placements below for deeper insight.

Heliocentric Astrology For Dion Fortune, born December 6, 1890 at 2:11 am in Llandudno, Wales

- Earth at 13 degrees Gemini 56
- Mercury at 17 degrees Capricorn 55
- Venus at 15 degrees Gemini 04
- Mars at 2 degrees Aries 38
- Jupiter at 18 degrees Aquarius 29
- Saturn at 10 degrees Virgo 42
- Uranus at 27 degrees Libra 40
- Neptune at 5 degrees Gemini 26
- Pluto at 6 degrees Gemini 54
- Chiron at 29 degrees Cancer 44

A free heliocentric ephemeris is available online. See horoscope: astroseek.com/heliocentric-ephemeris. Many computer programs will offer heliocentric astrology as an option. Solar Fire by Astrolabe is an excellent choice. See www.alabe.com for details.

—DIKKI-JO MULLEN

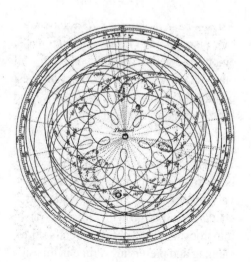

MOON GARDENING

BY PHASE

Sow, transplant, bud and graft   *Plow, cultivate, weed and reap*

NEW	First Quarter	FULL	Last Quarter	NEW
Plant above-ground crops with outside seeds, flowering annuals.	Plant above-ground crops with inside seeds.	Plant root crops, bulbs, biennials, perennials.		Do not plant.

BY PLACE IN THE ZODIAC

In general—plant and transplant crops that bear above ground when the Moon is in a watery sign: Cancer, Scorpio or Pisces. Plant and transplant root crops when the Moon is in Taurus or Capricorn; the other earthy sign, Virgo, encourages rot. The airy signs, Gemini, Libra and Aquarius, are good for some crops and not for others. The fiery signs, Aries, Leo and Sagittarius, are barren signs for most crops and best used for weeding, pest control and cultivating the soil.

♈

Aries—*barren, hot and dry.* Favorable for planting and transplanting beets, onions and garlic, but unfavorable for all other crops. Good for weeding and pest control, for canning and preserving, and for all activities involving fire.

♉

Taurus—*fruitful, cold and dry.* Fertile, best for planting root crops and also very favorable for all transplanting as it encourages root growth. Good for planting crops that bear above ground and for canning and preserving. Prune in this sign to encourage root growth.

♊

Gemini—*barren, hot and moist.* The best sign for planting beans, which will bear more heavily. Unfavorable for other crops. Good for harvesting and for gathering herbs.

♋

Cancer—*fruitful, cold and moist.* Best for planting crops that bear above ground and very favorable for root crops. Dig garden beds when the Moon is in this sign, and everything planted in them will flourish. Prune in this sign to encourage growth.

♌

Leo—*barren, hot and dry.* Nothing should be planted or transplanted while the Moon is in the Lion. Favorable for weeding and pest control, for tilling and cultivating the soil, and for canning and preserving.

♍

Virgo—*barren, cold and dry.* Good for planting grasses and grains, but unfavorable for other crops. Unfavorable for canning and preserving, but favorable for weeding, pest control, tilling and cultivating. Make compost when the Moon is in the Virgin and it will ripen faster.

≏

Libra—*fruitful, hot and moist*. The best sign to plant flowers and vines and somewhat favorable for crops that bear above the ground. Prune in this sign to encourage flowering.

♏

Scorpio—*fruitful, cold and moist*. Very favorable to plant and transplant crops that bear above ground, and favorable for planting and transplanting root crops. Set out fruit trees when the Moon is in this sign and prune to encourage growth.

♐

Sagittarius—*barren, hot and dry*. Favorable for planting onions, garlic and cucumbers, but unfavorable for all other crops, and especially unfavorable for transplanting. Favorable for canning and preserving, for tilling and cultivating the soil, and for pruning to discourage growth.

♑

Capricorn—*fruitful, cold and dry*. Very favorable for planting and transplanting root crops, favorable for flowers, vines, and all crops that bear above ground. Plant trees, bushes and vines in this sign. Prune trees and vines to strengthen the branches.

♒

Aquarius—*barren, hot and moist*. Favorable for weeding and pest control, tilling and cultivating the soil, harvesting crops, and gathering herbs. Somewhat favorable for planting crops that bear above ground, but only in dry weather or the seeds will tend to rot.

♓

Pisces—*fruitful, cold and moist*. Very favorable for planting and transplanting crops that bear above ground and favorable for flowers and all root crops except potatoes. Prune when the Moon is in the Fishes to encourage growth. Plant trees, bushes and vines in this sign.

Consult our Moon Calendar pages for phase and place in the zodiac circle. The Moon remains in a sign for about two and a half days. Match your gardening activity to the day that follows the Moon's entry into that zodiacal sign. For best results, choose days when the phase and sign are both favorable. For example, plant seeds when the Moon is waxing in a suitable fruitful sign, and uproot stubborn weeds when the Moon is in the fourth quarter in a barren sign.

NYSSA—THE CALL

An Excerpt From Cyndi Brannen's
Entering Hekate's Garden

The Garden of Hekate, the great Mother Goddess from whom all the world flows, is the spiritual home for the practice of pharmakeia, the ancient art, craft, and science of plant-spirit witchcraft. This practice uses botanicals for corporeal purposes, the crafting of magical formulations, and the art of transcending. It is a holistic art transmitted by Hekate and her witches for our use today. Enter her mysteries with the spirit of beginning—the spirit of the crossroads that we enter when we answer the call of Hekate to return to the practice of holistic plant-spirit witchcraft.

Hekate is the Triple Goddess of magick, medicine, and mystery. She is also the Mother of all practitioners of plant-spirit witchcraft. One of her daughters, the goddess Circe, is the mistress of plant-spirit medicine. The other, Medea, is the mistress of the Poison Path. Together, these three form the Triple Goddesses of our craft. Circe and Medea balance each other and represent the creative and destructive natures of the Green World. Connecting to the Triple Goddesses, and to other deities, botanicals, spirits, and correspondences, is natural for witches. It is unnatural and unhealthy when we deny ourselves these associations. These spirits, forces, energetics, and correspondences are as vital to us as air. As we are born knowing how to breathe, we come into this life hard-wired for connection. We are attuned to our souls. The knowledge flows freely within us, and between us and the external world, seen and unseen.

Reclaiming the practice of pharmakeia is a homecoming. We hear it in a whisper from Hekate, discover it in an unexpected key, marvel at it in a spell successfully cast. When we experience the feeling of being in flow, we have attuned ourselves and our souls. We are connecting to the spirits who work in our best interests. Our souls are recovered and our shadows healed, to become trusted companions rather than adversaries. When we begin the dance of the pharmaka, we enter into our truth and wholeness, confronting the illusion of separation that comes from the acts and laws of man. When you are ready to destroy this illusion, then you are prepared for pharmakeia.

The Green World has its own laws and masters. The plant spirits are ruled by the cycle of life-death-rebirth. They follow the principles of nature. We become attuned to the verdancy—the synergistic experience of the fiery soul that lives within all creatures throughout the Green World, also known as the Anima Mundi.

Pharmakeia is the holistic practice of plant-spirit witchcraft that incorporates the corporeal, the magical, and the spiritual. There is no division between the three. Pharmakeia breaks down the illusion of separation and reveals how the verdant world reflects the duality within us. Allopathic medicine, mainstream healthcare, would have us believe that plants only treat the physical self. Yet the truth is that this is a recent development in the practice of pharmakeia. If we open our spirits, minds, and hearts, we can hear the call of the Anima Mundi. Heed Hekate's call to enter her eternal garden.

Holistic Healing

The illusion of separation occurs when we separate magick from medicine. Allopathic healthcare has completely divorced spiritual aspects from practice.

It's something I ran into in my career as a health researcher. Only over the past few decades has the role of spirituality been taken seriously within mainstream healthcare, but there's still a long way to go before the sacred green fire is truly embraced yet again in mainstream treatment protocols. As you grow in your practice of pharmakeia, it becomes apparent that there is no separation between applications—botanicals work on the corporeal in conjunction with the spiritual. This is part of your reconnection to the eternal abilities of the witch as a practitioner of "medicine."

Recognizing botanicals for their medicinal properties—as the materia medica that they are—deepens our understanding. All plants are medicine. Witchcraft consists of working with medicine to heal whatever is broken and to create that which is whole. Shallow practice that avoids the true nature of botanicals as medicine prevents successful witchery, leaning more toward wishcraft than witchcraft.

The green fire burns bright—intimidating for certain, but holding so much power.

The word "medicine" comes from a Latin root word meaning "remedy" and the "art of healing." To the ancients, medicine was holistic rather than reductionist, as our modern mainstream healthcare system has become. Traditional systems of healing around the world, on the other hand, treat the whole person, including the spirit, when there is dis-ease. This is the path of pharmakeia.

Our society is suffering more and more, with ever-increasing amounts of pharmaceuticals being forced down our throats. While this sort of medicine may at times be necessary, it rarely treats the underlying spiritual ailments that give birth to their corporeal symptoms. Children who may be undergoing an awakening of their psychic abilities are force-fed drugs that may harm them forever. Adults who are in the grip of sadness are denied comfort and given pills instead. While there are many well-intentioned professionals in mainstream healthcare, the mechanism driving the whole system is profit, particularly that of pharmaceutical corporations.

When the patriarchy took hold of medical practice, the prime objective was to silence the healers who refused to conform. The long road from pharmakeia as the holistic practice of herbalism to what we now think of as "pharma" began when medicine was taken away from the healers by men of power. But now, we reclaim the power of pharmakeia as our right. It is our true medicine.

Practicing True Medicine

To banish, to connect, and to protect. To heal. To make ourselves whole. To share our healing with others. These are the skills of the botanical witch. This is our true medicine. It is through reconnection to the pharmakoi that we find our true power. Cleansing and protection through plant spirits are the two basic techniques of pharmakeia.

To understand how the magic of botanicals works, we turn to their origins and properties. Practitioners of pharmakeia seek to understand the underlying forces at work so as to strengthen their practice. Like Circe and Medea and all our witch ancestors, we find our strength in knowledge. Like us, plants are borne of Hekate. As such, we are remarkably similar. We are the soul made into body. The spiritual as corporeal. Our DNA is almost identical to that of plants. Botanicals were the first exhalation of the Mother. We rose from them with her second breath. In the physical sense, we evolved from the

Green World and are interdependent with it. The pharmakoi nourish us as we sustain them. They are the true medicine. Healing is the work of the pharmaka, the practitioner of holistic witchcraft herbalism.

Pharmakeia has been corrupted by profiteers so much that even using this ancient term to describe the practice of witchcraft as medicine is confusing. Contemplate that for a moment. The original definition of the word pharmakeia is both "medicine" and "a spell or potion." The original practice of pharmakeia was thus holistic, meaning that there was no separation between spirit and body. How different modern pharmacology would be if this approach had never been abandoned. Our spells and potions are healing. Not only do they reduce suffering; they create abundance. That is true health. The pharmakoi are the plant teachers, the over-spirits of each individual plant. We work with these spirits in their many forms, from imbibing their pure energy to consuming them. Pharmakeia is the medicine of life.

Pharmakeia is the merger of the scientific and the sacred. It is remembering that this is what medicine is, and that witches have always been the stewards of this power. Hekate as Anima Mundi, the World Soul, is infused in all life. Her fire runs through all of creation. Spiritually, this is known through experience. Physiologically, this is found in the carbon that infuses all life. Scientifically, we know that botanicals contain vital nutrients like antioxidants, stimulants, and vitamins in their corporeal selves. Spiritually, the same vital nourishers are found in their etheric beings. When we practice witchcraft as medicine, we summon both the physical properties and the spirits of the plants.

Witchcraft is the medicine that heals the spirit and nourishes the soul for those who walk this crooked path. It's not found in a pill or in a ball of light, but in the pungent scent of herbs, in the wild energy of the natural world, and under the pale moonlight. For centuries, our true medicine has been suppressed by others who sought to silence us. Now the time has come to reclaim it.

—CYNDI BRANNEN

Entering Hekate's Garden is available at redwheelweiser.com

Cyndi Brannen, PhD, *is a spiritual teacher, trained energetic healer, psychic, and herbalist. Merging her training in shamanism, tarot, past life work, meditation, and psychology, she teaches and writes about better living through witchcraft. Visit her at www. keepingherkeys.com*

The MOON Calendar

is divided into zodiac signs rather than the more familiar Gregorian calendar.

2021

2022

Bear in mind that new projects should be initiated when the Moon is waxing (from dark to full). When the Moon is on the wane (from full to dark), it is a time for storing energy and the wise person waits.

Please note that Moons are listed by day of entry into each sign. Quarters are marked, but as rising and setting times vary from one region to another, it is advisable to check your local newspaper, library or planetarium. *The Moon's Place is computed for Eastern Time.*

pisces
February 19 – March 20, 2021
Mutable Sign of Water ▽ Ruled by Neptune ♆

S	M	T	W	T	F	S
Ash-Nion-N *February 18 – March 17* Like the birch and rowan, the ash thrives high in exposed hills. It comes to leaf as late as May and loses it leaves by early October. The Greeks dedicated the ash tree to Poseidon, God of the sea, and sailors carried its wood as protection against the threat of drowning. In Northern Europe, the ash as Yggdrasil ⬇					Feb **19** Gemini	**20** *Collaborate*
21 *Journey through art*	**22** Cancer	**23**	**24** *Show how* Leo	**25**	**26** Virgo	**27** Chaste Moon
28 WANING Libra	Mar **1** Matronalia	**2** *Be gentle* Scorpio	**3**	**4** *See what is* Sagittarius	**5**	**6** *Do it* Capricorn
7	**8** *Watch the sky*	**9** Aquarius	**10**	**11** *Support charity* Pisces	**12**	**13** Aries
14 WAXING	**15** *Find the good*	**16** Taurus	**17**	**18** *Use words* Gemini	**19** Minerva's Day	**20** *Have faith*

is the World Tree connecting the Underworld, Earth and Heaven. The ash is associated with Odin (Woden), supreme among gods, who sought to increase his wisdom by means of extreme suffering. It was on the ash tree that he hanged himself as an offering to himself and thus gained the runes. It was also under this tree that the three Ladies of Fate stirred their pot which contained the destiny of all.

Witchery and the Legend of Brigadoon

Brigadoon: a place that is idyllic, unaffected by time, or remote from reality

–Merriam-Webster 2020

THE HIGHLANDS of Scotland, one of the most sparsely populated areas in Europe, are rich in history and magic. It is there that a village lies which neither appears on any maps or is even accessible except to the villagers who live there. In the 17th century, according to legend, it was known that many Witches and spirits loitered in the area. The minister in this elusive place decided to resolve the situation by asking for a miracle. The miracle was granted, but at a price. The request for a blessing was answered by a decree—that the village of Brigadoon would appear for only one day in each century.

For those who are very lucky, who believe that all things are possible, who believe hard enough, one day Brigadoon might be seen at dawn, rising out of the morning mist. It will disappear again at sunset for another hundred years. There might or might not be an entire village of Brigadoon. Yet for all who would follow the way of the Witch, what can be found may always be cherished and remembered. It is a reminder that it is possible to discover beauty, a lovely and magical place promised with the dawning of each day. As it disappears into the night, a reminder of other realities and possibilities lingers.

—ELAINE NEUMEIER

aries

March 21 – April 19, 2021

Cardinal Sign of Fire △ Ruled by Mars ♂

S	M	T	W	T	F	S
						Mar 20 Vernal Equinox

Alder-Fearn-F *March 18–April 14* The alder is found in thickets beside lakes, streams and rivers, favouring marshy conditions. When dried, the wood is water resistant. For centuries alder has provided pilings to serve as building foundations and charcoal derived from alder wood is superior to all others. The alder is associated with Bran, Celtic ↓

S	M	T	W	T	F	S
21 Cancer	**22**	**23** *Frolic* Leo	**24**	**25** *Dare the unknown* Virgo	**26**	**27** *Convene at midnight*
28 Seed Moon Libra	**29** WANING	**30** Scorpio	**31** *Carry something red*	**April 1** April Fools' Day Sagittarius	**2**	**3** *Enjoy solitude* Capricorn
4	**5** Aquarius	**6** *Evil is ignorance*	**7**	**8** Pisces	**9** *Seek the willow*	**10** Aries
11	**12** WAXING Taurus	**13**	**14**	**15** *Open your mind* Gemini	**16** *Open your heart*	**17** Cancer
18	**19**					

hero-God. In the *Voyage of Bran to the World Below*, Bran describes waking from a dream to find himself in the presence of a Goddess holding a silver branch. It was said that whistles made of the bark of the alder can conjure up winds. The alder will yield three dyes, red, green and brown. When the tree is felled the white interior will begin to bleed red.

YEAR OF THE METAL OX
February 12, 2021 – January 31, 2022

This is a Metal Ox year. Gentle and patient, the Ox, Cow or Water Buffalo, is beloved and respected in legends and art throughout Asia. The diligent Ox reaches its goals through sheer endurance. It's best to keep on Ox's good side though. When offended or betrayed the Buffalo can become infuriated, charging an adversary or problem with a rage that amounts to violence. This is rare though. Usually this faithful and humble one can be found pulling a plough or turning the water wheel. Ox is a good and stable friend who provides sustenance for others. The Metal, or White Ox, is charismatic and intuitive. An aura of spirituality combined with superb social skills surrounds those born in a Metal Ox year. With startling eloquence, they combine language skills with subtle humor to make a point. Throughout the year strong opinions concerning right and wrong are firmly held. Loyalty is important and a certain stubbornness prevails. It is wise to be observant and to develop outstanding accuracy and proficiency. The choices made and actions followed tend to leave lasting impressions on surroundings. Be aware of potential impacts and think things through before moving forward.

More information on the Elemental Animal can be found on our website at
http://TheWitchesAlmanac.com/almanac-extras/

Years of the Ox
1937, 1949, 1961, 1973, 1985, 1997, 2009, 2021, 2033

Illustration by Ogmios MacMerlin

taurus

April 20 – May 20, 2021
Fixed Sign of Earth ♉ Ruled by Venus ♀

S	M	T	W	T	F	S
		April 20 Leo	21	22 Virgo	23	24 *Enchant a stone* Libra
25	26 Hare Moon Scorpio	27 WANING	28 *Weave a fantasy* Sagittarius	29	30 Walpurgis Night Capricorn	May 1 Beltane
2 Aquarius	3	4	5 *Meet by the sea* Pisces	6	7 *Light a candle* Aries	8 White Lotus Day
9	10 *Cherish solitude* Taurus	11	12 WAXING Gemini	13 *Let spirit move you*	14	15 Cancer
16 *Bathe in sunlight*	17 Leo	18	19 Virgo	20		

Willow-Saille-S *April 15–May 12* Willows are magical trees with slender, pale silver-green leaves. In ancient Greece, the Goddess Hera was born under a willow on the island of Samos. In the underworld kingdom of Pluto and Persephone, Orpheus touched a willow branch and received the gift of eloquence. Willow groves are scared to Hecate, Goddess of Witchcraft. Medieval herbalists placed all willows under the rulership of the Moon. The willow is sacred to the Moon Goddess and her domains, the rivers and lakes.

For bringing the Fairies back to house which they have deserted

Fairies!—whatsoever sprite
Near about us dwells—
You who roam the hills at night,
You who haunt the dells—
Where you harbour, hear us!
By the Lady Hecate's might we cry you to come near us!

Whether ancient wrong (alack!),
Malice, or neglect
Angered you and made you pack
With so drear effect,
Hearts you shall not harden:
Bathe your hurts and come you back again to house and garden!

For oak and ash and thorn,
By the rowan tree,
This was done ere we were born:
Kith nor kin are we
Of the folk whose blindness
Shut you out with scathe and scorn and banished with unkindness

We do call you, hands entwined,
Standing at our door,
With the glowing hearth behind
And the wood before.
Thence, where you are lurking,
Back we bring you, bring and bind, with your own magic's working.

Lo, our best we give for cess,
Having naught above
Handsel of our happiness
Seizin of our love.—
Take it then, O fairies!
Homely gods that guard and bless—O little kindly lares!

Punch JANUARY 1914

gemini

May 21 – June 20, 2021
Mutable Sign of Air △ Ruled by Mercury ☿

S	M	T	W	T	F	S
Hawthorn-Uath-H *May 13–June 9* The hawthorn is a small tree that seldom exceeds 15 feet in height. Its long thorns provide protection for nesting birds, as well as self protection from grazing animals. The bark is dark grey and the pale pink or white blossoms exude a strong, unusual scent. ↓					May **21** *Sing the mist away* Libra	**22**
23	**24** Scorpio	**25** Total Lunar Eclipse ⇨	**26** Dyad Moon Sagittarius	**27** WANING Vesak Day ⇦	**28** Capricorn	**29** Oak Apple Day
30 Aquarius	**31**	June **1** *Suffer not a fool* Pisces	**2**	**3** *Break old habits* Aries	**4**	**5** Night of the Watchers
6 *Walk until weary* Taurus	**7**	**8** *Read the cards* Gemini	**9** Partial Solar Eclipse ⇨	**10**	**11** WAXING Cancer	**12**
13 Leo	**14** *Embrace your familiar*	**15**	**16** *Gather eight stones* Virgo	**17**	**18** *Revel in the wind* Libra	**19**
20 Scorpio	Hawthorn is so strongly associated with the Celtic May Eve festival that "may" is a folk name for the tree. Whitethorn is another name popular in Brittany, where the tree marks Fairy trysting places. Sacred hawthorns guard wishing wells in Ireland, where shreds of clothing are hung on the thorns to symbolize a wish made. Thorn trees are bewitched according to old legends. In some cultures, they served as protection and had a purifying power.					

Summer Solstice Sippin'

THERE'S NOTHING like celebrating the longest day of the year with a tall glass, filled with summer fruits and herbs. You can enjoy this drink throughout the whole season. You can even make it in those cold winter months, to remind you of warmer days.

Rosemary is the featured herb here. Associated with love, memory, stability and protection, it's the perfect addition for all sorts of food spells and kitchen magic.

This recipe serves eight. It's nonalcoholic, but there's an option to add rum or tequila to make this a cocktail.

Summer Sippin'
Serves 8
2 cups cold water
3/4 cup white sugar
2 sprigs fresh rosemary leaves, destemmed and chopped
2 cups lemon juice
1 medium watermelon, seeded and cubed
8 ounces tequila or white rum (optional)
8 cups ice cubes

Directions
Grab a saucepan and add the water and sugar. Bring to a rolling boil, over high heat. Stir until the sugar has completely dissolved. Add the chopped rosemary leaves, and give them a good stir. Pour the water, sugar, and rosemary into a large jar and let it steep for about an hour.

Add one cup of lemon juice and half the watermelon into a blender. Remember to use just the red flesh of the watermelon—no rind and no seeds.

Using a metal strainer or sieve to catch the rosemary leaves, pour the water, rosemary and sugar syrup into the blender. If you're making this a cocktail, this is where you'll add the alcohol. Pop on the lid and puree until smooth. Pour the blended mix into a large serving jug. Blend the rest of the lemon and watermelon and add to the jug.

Your Summer Sippin' is ready. Just add a couple of ice cubes to a glass and fill with the watermelon and rosemary blend. Keep any leftovers in the fridge for up to three days, although there probably won't be any leftovers!

—GWION RAVEN

cancer

June 21 – July 22, 2021

Cardinal Sign of Water ▽ Ruled by Moon ☽

CANCER

S	M	T	W	T	F	S
	June **21** Summer Solstice	**22** Sagittarius	**23** *Gather among the trees*	**24** Mead Moon Capricorn	**25** Midsummer ⇦ WANING	**26** Aquarius
27 *Only read and rest*	**28** Pisces	**29**	**30** *Change plans*	July **1** ◑ Aries	**2**	**3** *Take action* Taurus
4	**5** *Confront indecision* Gemini	**6**	**7** *Meet at the crossroads*	**8** *Roam the seaside* Cancer	**9** ●	**10** WAXING Leo
11 *As above so below*	**12**	**13** Virgo	**14** *Talk to the birds*	**15** *Seek your own kind* Libra	**16**	**17** ◐ Scorpio
18 *Expose your soul*	**19** *Bathe in the sea* Sagittarius	**20**	**21** *Honor Isis* Capricorn	**22**		

Oak-Duir-D June *10–July 7* Oaks grow taller and live longer than most other species of trees. Oaks range in height from 40 to 120 feet and can live as long as 250 years. The oak was sacred to Zeus, Jupiter, Thor and many lightning Gods. The Midsummer fires were fed with oak. In days past, the oak was the favoured tree for doors, in fact the name *Duir* means door. The oak was the sacred to the Druids, who would hold their rituals under the tree and harvest mistletoe from its boughs.

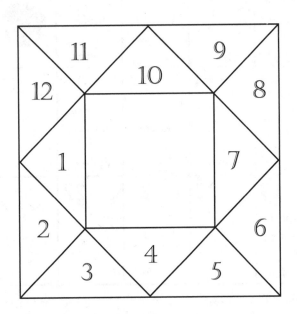

leo

July 23 – August 22, 2021

Fixed Sign of Fire △ Ruled by Sun ☉

LEO

S	M	T	W	T	F	S
Holly-Tinne-T *July 8–August 4* Holly is an evergreen growing as an under-shrub in many woods and forests. Some varieties, given space and opportunity, will grow to be 40 feet tall. The holly and the oak are the two trees representing the Divine Kings, oak representing the waxing year and holly ↓				Ancient Egyptian New Year ⇨	July **23** ◯ Wort Moon Aquarius	**24** WANING
25 Pisces	**26**	**27**	**28** Aries	**29** Bake bread	**30** Lughnassad Eve ⇨ Taurus	**31** ◗
Aug **1** Lammas	**2** Welcome a stranger Gemini	**3**	**4** Trust your senses Cancer	**5**	**6** Think of yourself	**7** Show joy Leo
8 ●	**9** WAXING Virgo	**10** Travel a new road	**11** Libra	**12**	**13** Diana's Day Scorpio	**14** Eat lemon
15 ◗	**16** Sagittarius	**17** Black Cat Appreciation Day	**18** Postpone action Capricorn	**19**	**20** Smile from ear to ear Aquarius	**21** Meet at owl time
22 ◖ Green Corn Moon Pisces	representing the waning cycle. The Celtic myth of Sir Gawain and the Green Knight has the two opponents meeting in combat at Midsummer and Midwinter. Gawain carries a club of oak. The Green Knight's weapon is a bough of holly. Holly had a strong association with divination in Northern Europe.					

57

PRIMOSES.—At Cockfield, Suffolk, there are none, nor, it is said, do they thrive whon planted, though they are numerous in all the surrounding villages, which do not apparently differ from Cockfield in soil.

The village legend says that here, too, they once were plentiful, but when Cockfield was depopulated by the plague, they also caught the infection and died, nor have they flourished since that time.—E.G.R. (Vol. VII., p 201.)

Choice Notes (Folklore from *Notes and Queries*), 1889.

virgo

August 23 – September 21, 2021

Mutable Sign of Earth ♍ Ruled by Mercury ☿

S	M	T	W	T	F	S
	Aug **23** WANING Aries	**24**	**25** Recall a dream	**26**	**27** Gather vervain Taurus	**28**
29 Gemini	**30** 🌓	**31** Practice astral projection	Sept **1** Moon rides low Cancer	**2**	**3** Wear gold Leo	**4**
5 Use no salt Virgo	**6** 🌑	**7** WAXING Libra	**8**	**9** A night of good fortune	**10** Ganesh Chaturthi Scorpio	**11**
12 A wishing day Sagittarius	**13** 🌗	**14** Capricorn	**15**	**16** Luck is yours Aquarius	**17** Trust your head	**18** Pisces
19 Gather for Esbat	**20** (Barley Moon)	**21** WANING Aries				

Hazel-Coll-C *August 5–September 1*

Unprepossessing to look at, more a spreading bush than a tree, the hazel rarely exceeds 12 feet in height. The magical significance of hazel crosses cultural lines, for it appears in the lore of Northern Europe, Southern Europe and the Near East. The staff of the Roman God Mercury was of hazel wood. The medieval magician's wand was traditionally cut from the hazel tree and ancient Irish heralds carried white hazel wands. Forked hazel sticks were employed by dowsers to discover underwater sources, mineral deposits and buried treasure. Celtic lore has it that the hazel nut is an emblem of wisdom, imparting the art of poetry for all that know how to partake of its concentration of wisdom. Legend has it that there were nine hazel trees that hung over the pool where the sacred salmon lived.

The following spell is said to be still used by some country maidens in Suffolk:—

A clover of two, if you put in yr shoe,
The next man you meet in field or lane
Will be yr husband, or one of the name.

To ascertain whether her pretended lovers really love her or not, the maiden takes an apple pip, and naming one of her followers, puts the pip in the fire. If it makes a noise in bursting, from the heat, it is a proof of love; but if it is consumed without a crack, she is fully satisfied that there is no real regard towards her in the person named.

libra

September 22 – October 22, 2021
Cardinal Sign of Air ♎ Ruled by Venus ♀

LIBRA

S	M	T	W	T	F	S
Vine-Muin-M *September 2– September 29* Celtic scholars agree that vine refers to blackberry bramble bush. The sacred nature of the black-berry is evidenced in old tales. A loop of blackberry bramble served as a source of healing. Traditional ↓			Sept **22** Autumnal Equinox	**23** *Eat barley* Taurus	**24**	**25** *Open your third eye* Gemini
26	**27** *Let your instinct guide you*	**28** ◖ Cancer	**29**	**30** *No nonsense* Leo	Oct **1**	**2** *Laughter cleanses*
3 *Pick apples* Virgo	**4**	**5** *Write to a past love* Libra	**6** ●	**7** WAXING Scorpio	**8** *Fashion not fad*	**9** Sagittarius
10	**11** *Bury an offering in the Earth* Capricorn	**12** ◗	**13** *Savor secrets* Aquarius	**14**	**15** *Trust reason* Pisces	**16**
17 *Observe the stars*	**18** Aries	**19** *Consult the spirit board*	**20** Harvest Moon	**21** WANING Taurus	**22**	

rites involved passing a baby through the loop three times to secure good health. One ancient legend tells how blackberries gathered and eaten within the span of the waxing moon at harvest time assured protection from the force of evil runes. For refuge in times of danger, one need only creep under a bramble bush. In rural regions of France and the British Isles, even to the present day, it is considered dangerous to eat blackberries. The reason given in Brittany is the fruit belongs to Fairies and they resent it when mortals presume to taste the magical berries.

La Lechuza

Evil Spirit of the Night

LA LECHUZA (the owl) refers to a woman who turns into an owl in Mexican-American folklore. La Lechuza begins as a human who sells her soul to the devil to become a bruja (witch), seen as a gigantic owl with the face of a hag.

The Mexican-American communities of the southwestern United States have many stories about this menace. She is sometimes described as having a wingspan of 12 feet and is capable of carrying off a grown man. She is very intelligent, finding many ways to create opportunities to locate those she wishes to harass or devour.

La Lechuza often perches on the roof of her intended victim and cries like a human infant to draw the person outside, where he or she can be pounced upon, or whistles incessantly until the person cannot stand it any longer. Children are instructed that, should they encounter La Lechuza, they must not look into her eyes or she will steal their souls while they sleep.

She is said to have the power to control weather, to bring thunder and lightning to confuse her prey. She can cause car batteries to die and seems to target those who drive while inebriated. If especially hungry, she will try to force a car off the road to get at the people inside.

Many parallels to La Lechuza exist in the folklore of other cultures. Some Native American tribes consider the owl to be a harbinger of death. In living Cherokee folk practice, the screech owl in the middle of the night means that someone in the family will die unless you immediately tie knots in the corners of all bed sheets. La Lechuza also has similarities to the ancient Greek furies or harpies, Macha of the Celtic countries and the fetch in Witchcraft lore as well as the skin-walkers of the Navajo, Hopi and Zuni tribes of the Southwest.

There are methods to protect yourself from the giant bird. One practice involves reciting many prayers while rubbing a fresh hen's egg over the body of the person who heard or saw the vicious creature, but most people who encounter her do not survive. She is immune to guns or other weapons but another defense of sorts is to curse at her, though this may not be very effective. The best defense is to use salt. Sprinkle it around your doors and windows, or as a last resort you can even throw a handful of it at La Lechuza.

—ZANONI SILVERKNIFE

Zanoni Silverknife entered the Summerland in Spring 2020, just before the 2021 Almanac went to press. We are honored to present this article, and grateful for the light she held out for us and countless others.

scorpio
October 23 – November 21, 2021
Fixed Sign of Water ▽ Ruled by Pluto ♀

SCORPIVS

S	M	T	W	T	F	S
	Ivy-Gort-G *September 30–October 27* When ivy trails along the ground, it remains weak and does not produce fruit. When it climbs using a tree or wall for support, it grows increasingly stronger, putting out flowers in Autumn and berries in Spring. Its botanical name, hedera helix, describes ivy's spiral form, for *helix* means "to turn around." The rich deep evergreen color ⬇					Oct **23** Gemini
24	**25** *Bake a pie* Cancer	**26**	**27** *Silence before a storm*	**28** Leo	**29** *Part the veil*	**30** Virgo
31 Samhain Eve	Nov **1** Hallowmas Libra	**2** *Lose not substance for shadow*	**3** Scorpio	**4**	**5** WAXING Sagittarius	**6** *Be evasive*
7 *Heed a whim* Capricorn	**8**	**9** *Take pride* Aquarius	**10**	**11**	**12** *Polish the silver* Pisces	**13** *Gaze into the looking glass*
14 Aries	**15** *Wear violet*	**16** Hecate's Night Taurus	**17**	**18** Partial Lunar Eclipse ⇨	**19** Snow Moon	**20** WANING Gemini
21	and climbing action inspired the ancients to identify ivy with immortality, resurrection and rebirth. The classical Gods of wine, the Greek Dionysus and the Roman Bacchus, are often depicted wearing crowns of ivy. Ivy came to symbolize fidelity and one perfect leaf collected when the Moon was one day old was a useful amulet in matters of love. Ivy ale is a highly intoxicating brew that was a medieval favorite. An ivy bush is still a sign of a tavern in the British Isles.					

Notable Quotations

THE SUN

I cannot endure to waste anything so precious as autumnal sunshine by staying in the house.

Nathaniel Hawthorne,
The American Notebooks

You can't use your hand to force the sun to set.

Nigerian Proverb

O, Sunlight! The most precious gold to be found on Earth.

Roman Payne

For a dark street, sunshine is most welcome; for a wounded soul, love is most welcome!

Mehmet Murat ildan

Turn your face to the sun and the shadows fall behind you.

Maori Proverb

Don't sell the sun to buy a candle.

Jewish Proverb

The sun,--the bright sun, that brings back, not light alone, but new life, and hope, and freshness to man--burst upon the crowded city in clear and radiant glory. Through costly-coloured glass and paper-mended window, through cathedral dome and rotten crevice, it shed its equal ray.

Charles Dickens, Oliver Twist

O, Delian king, whose light-producing eye views all within, and all beneath the sky."

Orphic hymn to Apollo

Keep your face to the sun and you will never see the shadows."

Helen Keller

What sunshine is to flowers, smiles are to humanity. These are but trifles, to be sure; but scattered along life's pathway, the good they do is inconceivable.

Joseph Addison

Quotes compiled by Isabel Kunkle.

sagittarius

November 22 – December 20, 2021

Mutable Sign of Fire △ Ruled by Jupiter ♃

S	M	T	W	T	F	S
	Nov **22** Secure seeds for the birds Cancer	**23**	**24** Do nothing Leo	**25**	**26** Cook for family Virgo	**27**
28	**29** Pursue old pleasures Libra	**30**	Dec **1** Buy a blanket Scorpio	**2**	**3** Total Solar Eclipse ⇨ Sagittarius	**4**
5 An early frost WAXING Capricorn	**6** Friends are loved	**7** Friends bring comfort Aquarius	**8**	**9** Indulge yourself Pisces	**10**	**11** Aries
12	**13**	**14** Seek out mistletoe Taurus	**15** Read the runes	**16** Fairy Queen Eve Gemini	**17** Saturnalia	**18** Oak Moon
19 WANING Cancer	**20** Avoid the vulgar					

Reed-Ngetal-NG *October 18–November 24* The reed thrives in streams and marshes. Its other names—marsh-elder and guelder-rose—reveal an affinity for Europe's low-lying coastal regions. The folklore of Northern Europe has little regard for the reed, other than as a water-loving plant through which the winds play and may make sounds that convey esoteric messages. But in the more sun-kissed regions, reeds—slender and delicate, steadfast and useful—play significant roles in various myths. In ancient Egypt, the tropical reed inspired the design of the royal scepter, and arrows cut from its stalk were symbols of the pharaoh's power. In Greece, another variety of reed played a role in Pan's pursuit of the lovely chaste Syrinx. Pan pursued the nymph from mountain to river, where she eluded him by becoming a reed. The God fashioned the reeds into the first set of Pan pipes.

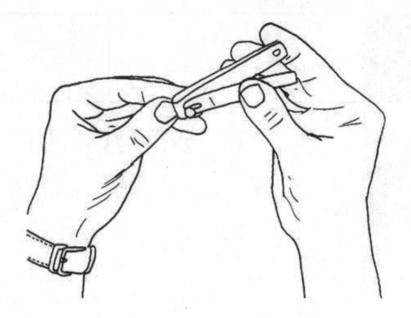

Cutting Nails

THERE IS a superstition also respecting cutting the nails…

To cut them on a Tuesday is thought particularly auspicious. Indeed, if we are to believe an old rhyming saw on this subject, every day of the week is endowed with its several and peculiar virtue, if the nails are invariably cut on that day and no other. The lines are as follow:

Cut them on Monday, you cut them for health;

Cut them on Tuesday, you cut them for wealth;

Cut them on Wednesday, you cut them for news;

Cut them on Thursday, a new pair of shoes;

Cut them on Friday, you cut them for sorrow;

Cut them on Saturday, see your true-love to-morrow;

Cut them on Sunday, the devil will be with you all the week.

Forby, VOL.II, P. 410.

capricorn

December 21 2021 – January 19, 2022
Cardinal Sign of Earth ♀ Ruled by Saturn ♄

S	M	T	W	T	F	S
		Dec **21** ❄ Winter Solstice Leo	**22** *Gaze into a fire*	**23**	**24** *Find a hidden way* Virgo	**25**
26 Libra	**27**	**28** Scorpio	**29** *Cherish privacy*	**30** Sagittarius	**31** *Live wild*	Jan **1** *Turn a penny* Capricorn
2	**3** WAXING Aquarius	**4**	**5** *Be vulnerable* Pisces	**6**	**7** *Venture now*	**8** *Beware of vampires* Aries
9	**10** Feast of Janus ⇐ Taurus	**11** *Hold friends dear*	**12**	**13** *Dance with abandon* Gemini	**14** *Enjoy tea by the fire*	**15** Cancer
16	**17** Wolf Moon	**18** WANING Leo	**19** *Rest with a book*			

Elder-Ruis-R *November 25–December 22* Although elder likes moist soil, it grows everywhere if sheltered from the wind. Once permission has been asked and a twig of elder secured, it will banish evil spirits and may be hung or worn as an amulet. Elder flowers, dried while the Moon waxes from dark to full, are a potent love charm. The berries gathered at Summer Solstice afford protection from all unexpected dangers, including accidents and lightning strikes. Beyond its subtle gifts, the elder offers healing for a variety of ailments. Its leaves are an effective insect repellent; its close grained wood finds favor with carpenters; its berries provide a deep purple dye as well as culinary treats and the renowned elderberry wine. Hans Christian Andersen's tale of Elder Mother who becomes a beautiful maiden captures the spirit of ancient lore.

The Dog, the Cock and the Fox

A dog and a cock having struck up an acquaintance went out on their travels together. Nightfall found them in a forest, so the cock, flying up on a tree, perched among the branches, while the dog dozed below at the foot. As the night passed away and the day dawned, the cock, according to his custom, set up a shrill crowing.

A fox, hearing him and thinking to make a meal of him, came and stood under the tree and thus addressed him: "Thou art a good little bird and most useful to thy fellow creatures. Come down, then, that we may sing and rejoice together."

The cock replied; "Go, my good friend, to the foot of the tree, and call the church elders to toll the bell." But as the Fox went to call them, the dog jumped out in a moment, seized the fox, and made an end of him.

Moral: They who lay traps for others are often caught by their own bait.

aquarius

January 20, 2022 – February 18, 2022

Fixed Sign of Air △ Ruled by Uranus ♅

S	M	T	W	T	F	S
Birch-Beth-B *December 24–January 20* Few trees figure more prominently in the folklore of Northern Europe than the birch. Called the tree of inception, the birch is self sowing in forming new groves and is one of the earliest trees to put out leaves in Spring. Deemed sacred to Thor, Norse ↓				Jan **20** Virgo	**21**	**22** *Promise nothing* Libra
23	**24** *A test*	**25** ◑ Scorpio	**26**	**27** Sagittarius	**28** *Write a poem*	**29** Capricorn
30	**31** Oimelc Eve ⇨ Aquarius	Feb **1** ● 	**2** Chinese New Year ⇦ Pisces	**3** WAXING Candlemas ⇦	**4** *Grant a wish* Aries	**5**
6 *Guard possesions* Taurus	**7**	**8** ◐ 	**9** *Avoid fear* Gemini	**10**	**11** *A day to rejoice* Cancer	**12**
13 *Drink spring water*	**14** Leo	**15** Lupercalia	**16** ◯ Storm Moon	**17** WANING Virgo	**18** *Behold nature*	

God of thunder and lightning, the birch symbolizes youth. Its uncanny nature links the tree with Witchcraft. Birch is the wood of broomsticks, flying transport to the Sabbat gatherings. Birch turns up in many cultures. The Dakota Sioux burn birch bark to discourage thunder. Scandinavians carry a dried young leaf for good luck on the first day of a new job. Basque Witches use birch oil to anoint love candles. A birch grove guarded the house and land in colonial New England. Birch log smoke purifies the surroundings.

TAROT'S THE HERMIT

THE HERMIT may appear in the Tarot as one of Death's victims in his Dance. Alternatively, one of the Hermit's other titles, *Rerum Edax* "Devourer of Things," and other versions of his trump such as the one represented here depicting him carrying an hour glass instead of a lantern, indicate that his true identity may be all-devouring Time, portrayed in the image of the Greco-Roman god Kronos-Saturn. Warned by a prophecy that one of his sons would supplant him on the throne of heaven, Kronos began swallowing his children as soon as his wife Rhea gave birth to them. Rhea, however, finally foiled her husband's schemes by presenting him with stones wrapped in baby clothes to swallow. As a result, one of Kronos's sons, Zeus, grew to manhood, wrested the crown from him and banished him to rule the Isles of the Blessed forever. Basically this card represents Time and Old Age, and therefore all things, good or bad, associated with these matters.

Excerpted from Dame Fortune's Wheel Tarot—A Pictorial Key *by Paul Huson, published by The Witches' Almanac.*

pisces

February 19 – March 20, 2022

Mutable Sign of Water ▽ Ruled by Neptune ♆

S	M	T	W	T	F	S
	Rowan-Luis-L *January 21–February 17* The bright red berries of the mountain ash give this tree its Scottish name rowan from Gaelic rudha-an, the red one. An older and more romantic names is *luisliu*, flame or delight of the eye. Other names for the rowan are whitebeam, quickbeam or quicken and Witchwood. The latter possibly derives from the Anglo-Saxon root *wic*, meaning ↓					Feb **19** Libra
20	**21** Scorpio	**22** *Feel your power*	**23** ◑ Sagittarius	**24**	**25** *Do not conform* Capricorn	**26**
27 *Perform divination* Aquarius	**28**	Mar **1** *Spend time alone* Pisces	**2** ●	**3** WAXING Matronalia ⇦ Aries	**4** *Cast a spell*	**5**
6 *Embrace music* Taurus	**7**	**8** *Change old habits* Gemini	**9** *Breathe deeply*	**10** ◐	**11** *Contact family* Cancer	**12**
13 Leo	**14** *Cast a healing spell*	**15**	**16** *Prepare ritual candles* Virgo	**17**	**18** Ⓞ Chaste Moon Libra	**19** WANING Minerva's Day
20 *Spirits fly* Scorpio	pliable. The Druids would capture spirits in a wattle of rowan twigs to compel them to answer difficult questions. All across Northern Europe it is the custom to plant rowan trees near farm buildings to gain the favor of Thor and ensure safety for stored crops and animals from storm damage. A necklace of rowan beads enlivened the wearer and twigs were carried as protective charms. In Ireland the rowan tree was a sacred tree associated with the fire feast Candlemas.					

The Evolution
of the Magician

MAGIC in its primitive stage appears crude to present day ceremonialists. The use of stones and twigs in a ritual for crop fertilization, or the use of sacrifice in a healing rite seem totally unnecessary to us.

With the medieval European concept of the elements, brought to us by the alchemists of the times, came a whole new view of magical ritual based on the quartering of a whole. The four quarters of the universe, having the four elements as attributions, became the new setting for the temple. The use of the cardinal cross became more common, lending itself as a doorway to an infinite number of attributions ranging from colors to Godforms. The use of the double-cubed altar and the black and white checked floor of the temple are external reflections of the psychological base of the magician. The Cup, Wand, Sword and Pentacle represent the body of the magician as the universe. The microcosm becomes the macrocosm through the vibration of the four.

The Piscean age represents sacrifice for the sake of the whole. The family (being a reflection of four; Mother, Father, Child and Family unit) is a Piscean concept having its roots in the element of water. Members of society sacrificed themselves for the sake of others. The sense of working for the whole and the ignoring of the individual was, and still is, a very common attitude.

We are moving into the age of Aquarius, but few of us are willing to lay down our Piscean tools and beliefs and take that leap into a new home. The Aquarian age will bring a sense of individualization on the physical plane along with a true feeling of union on a higher plane. The mixed energies of Saturn and Uranus can lead to some difficulty in breaking away from old structures, but freedom will become an obsession with society, and people will make a move into the tide of air.

The magician will find that the concepts and methods employed in the Piscean ritual of yesterday will seem as crude as the primitive magician using stones and twigs. The obsolete employment of the four tools will be replaced by the use of color and sound vibration. The senses will play a much more important role on the path to transcendence. The sense of hearing (being attributed to Saturn) will be of the most importance. Secrets long forgotten from the age of Gemini will be rediscovered as the use of sound waves becomes the tool for the magician of tomorrow.

–From *The Emerald Star*,
volume 2, no.1, ©1980

Awake, Awake O Sleeper

of the Land of Shadows.

Wake! Expand!

Wm. Blake

DION FORTUNE

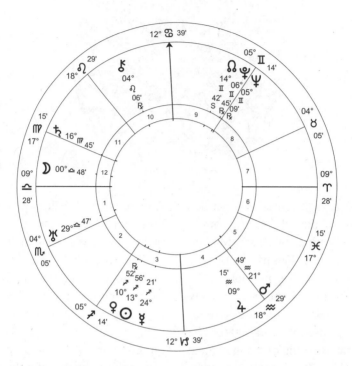

DION FORTUNE, one of the most significant contributors to the development of Witchcraft as it exists today, is the celebrity profile chosen for this fiftieth anniversary of the Witches' Almanac. Her inspirational and instructive legacy of metaphysical writings spans ceremonial magic, occultism, the Qabalah and Spiritualism.

Dion Fortune was born Violet Mary Firth on the December 6, 1890 at 2:11 a.m. in Llandudno, Wales into a wealthy upper middle class British family. Her paternal grandfather made his fortune in the steel industry in Sheffield, Yorkshire. It was he who coined the family motto, "*Deo non Fortuna*," which translates as, "God, not Fortune." Young Violet eventually adapted her nomme de plume, Dion Fortune, from this motto. Her parents were Christian Scientists. Her father, a lawyer and doctor, practiced alternative medicine in his hydrotherapy clinic in North Wales. Dion Fortune's mother encouraged her daughter in exploring trance mediumship and psychic healing.

Throughout her life Dion Fortune would return to her parents' home. In her horoscope, this privileged but unconventional and influential family background is indicated by the placement of Jupiter, accidentally exalted in her fourth house in Aquarius. Jupiter is part of a grand trine in Air signs formed with her Mars also in Aquarius, her Ascendant, Moon and Uranus in Libra and a Neptune Pluto conjunction along with the North Node of the Moon in Gemini. This powerful and favorable astrological pattern reveals great creativity, a progressive outlook and an ability to attune to higher planes of awareness.

Dion Fortune claimed that the concepts she shared were taught to her by spiritual beings called ascended masters during deep meditation and trance sessions. Her Sun, Mercury and Venus are in Sagittarius in her third house. This configuration shows excellent communication skills and scholarship, indicating her prolific talent as a writer.

She published two books of poetry as a teenager. Her seven metaphysical novels with occult themes and esoteric teachings are drawn from her life experiences. She established a group which survived her for many years called the Society (or Fraternity) of the Inner Light with centers in London and Glastonbury.

Dion Fortune had a flamboyant, fiery and outspoken personality, typical of a Sagittarius Sun. Her assertiveness created friction with many other prominent metaphysical practitioners of her era. Eventually she retired from group leadership to immerse herself in her writing, as indicated by her Moon's position, waning in the last quarter and in her twelfth house.

Chiron in her tenth house in Leo shows a career focus on health as well as teaching. A vegetarian, she started a company which sold soy milk products while she was very young. Her Saturn in Virgo in the eleventh house further describes this interest in health and her motivation to share wellness principles with her community.

She was also skilled in working with poultry. While still in her teens, she taught caring for poultry at the Horticultural College in Wiltshire, an institution dedicated to schooling troubled girls. It was there that she claimed to have been

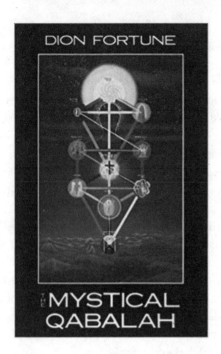

DION FORTUNE

THE MYSTICAL QABALAH

the victim of psychic manipulation by the school's warden, Lillias Hamilton. Following the resulting breakdown, Dion Fortune's classic work *Psychic Self Defense* was written.

Her Mars in Aquarius trine Uranus in Libra suggests her fascination with psychology. In her twenties she studied Freud, Adler and Jung at The University of London. While working as a counselor in a mental health clinic, she met the Irish occultist and Freemason Theodore Moriarty. He inspired the character of Dr. Taverner, the heroic figure in Dr. Taverner's Secrets, one her most popular novels. Her North Node and Pluto in her ninth house indicate the uplifting and transformative impact the university environment had on her.

In 1927 Dion Fortune married Dr. Tom Penry-Evans. Her Venus is retrograde, suggesting a troubled marriage. They had no children. It is generally thought she preferred an unconsummated relationship, with the goal of directing the energy of the libido into awakening the kundalini and higher consciousness. The couple honeymooned in Glastonbury where her husband apparently first realized the extent of what the immersion in occultism would mean to their life together. Eventually Penry-Evans asked for a divorce to marry another woman.

With retrograde Neptune in Gemini in her eighth house opposed by the retrograde Venus, Dion Fortune had strong passions expressed in secretive, subtle and unconventional ways. Combined with her natal Libra influences, this suggests seeking an equal balance between male and female energies. Her writings about powerful goddess worship, such as *The Sea Priestess* are an expression of this.

During World War II Dion Fortune wrote *the Magical Battle For Britain* in which she detailed building psychic protection against the negative occult practices shaping Europe at the time. In Sybil Leek's *Diary of a Witch*, Sybil refers to how the Witches of England gathered together to focus their powers on turning back the Nazis. Although they succeeded in this work, many great British occultists were destroyed, completely drained of their vitality, according to Sybil. This suggests a reference to Dion Fortune's death. She became very ill in 1945 and had to cancel an appearance at an important winter solstice event in December. She died in London at age 55 on January 6, 1946 of leukemia.

—DIKKI-JO MULLEN

DION FORTUNE
Born December 6, 1890
at 2:11 am GMT in Llandudno, Wales

Data Table
Tropical Placidus Houses

Sun 13 Sagittarius 56—3rd house

Moon 00 Libra 48—12th house

Mercury 24 Sagittarius 21—3rd house

Venus 10 Sagittarius 52' (retrograde)—3rd house

Mars 21 Aquarius 49—5th house

Jupiter 9 Aquarius 15—4th house

Saturn 16 Virgo 45—11th house

Uranus 29 Libra 47—1st house

Neptune 5 Gemini 09' (retrograde)—8th house

Pluto 6 Gemini 45 (retrograde)—9th house

Chiron 4 Leo 06 (retrograde)—10th house

North Moon Node 14 Gemini 42—9th house

Ascendant (rising sign) is 9 Libra 28

Wild Swan

Taking Flight

THE OTHER DAY I saw a wild swan for the first time since I moved back to the Midwest. It was a swan couple and I had forgotten just how large and magnificent they can be. The profundity of seeing them at that moment was not lost on me, for just an instant before I had received an amazing insight in which the spiritual study of over twenty years came full circle and revealed itself in such simplified clarity that it was a complete revelation.

Magical people come from different walks of life, from all over the planet, yet weave similar magic with similar threads. Some of these threads go by many names but nevertheless seem to be pretty much the same thing: hedge riding, trancework, plane walking, out of body experiences, working with the veil, astral projection, planes of consciousness, shamanic journeying,

wakeful dreaming, the ethers and more. Although I've been working with these threads for longer, it was approximately twenty years ago that I started consciously using entheogens to help me with this work. After a multiyear stint on an Indian reservation working daily with peyote, it only seemed natural that when I did finally turn to my European roots, the baneful entheogens of my ancestors called to me.

Late last Spring, after pondering how to make what the plants have taught me more accessible to others, the idea of making gourmet chocolate truffles infused with nightshades suddenly came to me. Once I had that thought and decided to act on it everything came together easily and quickly. Before I knew it I was off and running with my sacred plant medicine truffle business!

Learning from plants

Entheogenic plants are tools to help humans learn to go places that are inaccessible without their help. They are also teachers: initially humans need the plants' help to see and comprehend many things, even before learning what to do with them. Everyone who works with them will continue to level up with the plants. They always have more to teach but their teachings are like building blocks. When you are ready for more, the plants will give you more.

Eventually with practice and repetition we no longer need to ingest the plants to get to these places or do these things, but the plants are not one trick ponies. They have so much to show and teach—to stop ingesting them because you think you have already mastered what the plants can share is to greatly underestimate the potential of their teachings.

Consciousness

The more conscious you are during an experience, the more you can get and retain from it. What I love most about the nightshades in particular is that they allow me to practice all that I learned with peyote, but with greater clarity and consciousness. In other words, these plants can take you to the same places and show you the same things that hallucinogenic entheogens do, but the nightshades are able to do so without the hallucinations, and without getting a person high. In fact, I have found that I am able to keep complete mental clarity while walking the many and varied planes with the nightshades inside of me.

It's not uncommon that the first time a person tries one of my truffles they seem to have a hard time letting go of control or of their expectations of what they think should happen. Consequently, they end up missing much of the plants' influence. You need to allow the plant to become one with you—a merging needs to happen to really feel a plant spirit's presence. A lot of those first timers end up getting there after an hour or so, but this kind of work takes practice.

After you let go, you also need to learn to stay present. That may sound like a contradiction, but it is not. Do not completely let go and let the experience take you where it may. When you cannot remain in conscious presence after letting go, you become a passive entity at the mercy of whatever you may encounter. You still need to steer even when you're on another plane and the plants help you to do so. Without your own conscious participation, you are basically spacing out, just floating around like a feather and dancing in whatever up current or spirit may catch you. That might sound relaxing and fun in itself, but why be the feather when you can be the swan?

—SEAMUS BLACK

Find these delightful truffles at Emporium Black *on Facebook*

2021 SUNRISE AND SUNSET TIMES

Providence—San Francisco—Sydney—London

	Sunrise				Sunset			
	Prov	**SF**	**Syd**	**Lon**	**Prov**	**SF**	**Syd**	**Lon**
Jan 5	7:13 AM	7:26 AM	5:51 AM	8:05 AM	4:28 PM	5:04 PM	8:08 PM	4:06 PM
15	7:11 AM	7:24 AM	6:00 AM	7:59 AM	4:39 PM	5:14 PM	8:07 PM	4:20 PM
25	7:04 AM	7:19 AM	6:10 AM	7:49 AM	4:51 PM	5:25 PM	8:03 PM	4:37 PM
Feb 5	6:54 AM	7:10 AM	6:21 AM	7:32 AM	5:05 PM	5:37 PM	7:56 PM	4:56 PM
15	6:41 AM	6:59 AM	6:31 AM	7:14 AM	5:18 PM	5:48 PM	7:46 PM	5:15 PM
25	6:27 AM	6:47 AM	6:40 AM	6:54 AM	5:30 PM	5:58 PM	7:35 PM	5:33 PM
Mar 5	6:14 AM	6:35 AM	6:47 AM	6:37 AM	5:40 PM	6:06 PM	7:25 PM	5:47 PM
15	6:58 AM	7:21 AM	6:55 AM	6:15 AM	6:51 PM	7:16 PM	7:12 PM	6:04 PM
25	6:40 AM	7:05 AM	7:02 AM	5:52 AM	7:02 PM	7:25 PM	6:58 PM	6:21 PM
Apr 5	6:22 AM	6:49 AM	6:11 AM	6:27 AM	7:14 PM	7:35 PM	5:44 PM	7:39 PM
15	6:06 AM	6:35 AM	6:18 AM	6:05 AM	7:25 PM	7:44 PM	5:31 PM	7:56 PM
25	5:51 AM	6:21 AM	6:26 AM	5:44 AM	7:36 PM	7:53 PM	5:19 PM	8:13 PM
May 5	5:37 AM	6:10 AM	6:33 AM	5:26 AM	7:47 PM	8:03 PM	5:09 PM	8:29 PM
15	5:26 AM	6:00 AM	6:40 AM	5:09 AM	7:58 PM	8:11 PM	5:01 PM	8:44 PM
25	5:18 AM	5:53 AM	6:47 AM	4:56 AM	8:07 PM	8:20 PM	4:55 PM	8:58 PM
June 5	5:12 AM	5:49 AM	6:54 AM	4:47 AM	8:16 PM	8:27 PM	4:52 PM	9:11 PM
15	5:11 AM	5:48 AM	6:59 AM	4:44 AM	8:21 PM	8:32 PM	4:52 PM	9:18 PM
25	5:13 AM	5:50 AM	7:01 AM	4:45 AM	8:23 PM	8:34 PM	4:54 PM	9:20 PM
July 5	5:18 AM	5:54 AM	7:01 AM	4:52 AM	8:22 PM	8:33 PM	4:58 PM	9:17 PM
15	5:25 AM	6:01 AM	6:58 AM	5:02 AM	8:17 PM	8:29 PM	5:03 PM	9:09 PM
25	5:34 AM	6:08 AM	6:53 AM	5:15 AM	8:09 PM	8:23 PM	5:10 PM	8:57 PM
Aug 5	5:45 AM	6:18 AM	6:45 AM	5:31 AM	7:57 PM	8:12 PM	5:17 PM	8:40 PM
15	5:55 AM	6:26 AM	6:35 AM	5:47 AM	7:44 PM	8:00 PM	5:24 PM	8:21 PM
25	6:05 AM	6:35 AM	6:23 AM	6:03 AM	7:28 PM	7:47 PM	5:31 PM	8:00 PM
Sept 5	6:16 AM	6:44 AM	6:09 AM	6:20 AM	7:10 PM	7:31 PM	5:38 PM	7:36 PM
15	6:27 AM	6:52 AM	5:55 AM	6:36 AM	6:53 PM	7:15 PM	5:45 PM	7:13 PM
25	6:37 AM	7:01 AM	5:41 AM	6:52 AM	6:36 PM	7:00 PM	5:52 PM	6:50 PM
Oct 5	6:48 AM	7:10 AM	6:28 AM	7:08 AM	6:19 PM	6:45 PM	6:59 PM	6:27 PM
15	6:59 AM	7:19 AM	6:15 AM	7:25 AM	6:02 PM	6:30 PM	7:07 PM	6:06 PM
25	7:10 AM	7:29 AM	6:03 AM	7:42 AM	5:48 PM	6:17 PM	7:15 PM	5:45 PM
Nov 5	7:24 AM	7:40 AM	5:52 AM	7:02 AM	5:33 PM	6:05 PM	7:25 PM	4:25 PM
15	6:36 AM	6:51 AM	5:44 AM	7:19 AM	4:23 PM	4:57 PM	7:35 PM	4:10 PM
25	6:48 AM	7:01 AM	5:39 AM	7:35 AM	4:17 PM	4:51 PM	7:44 PM	3:58 PM
Dec 5	6:58 AM	7:11 AM	5:38 AM	7:49 AM	4:14 PM	4:49 PM	7:53 PM	3:52 PM
15	7:07 AM	7:18 AM	5:39 AM	8:00 AM	4:14 PM	4:51 PM	8:00 PM	3:50 PM
25	7:12 AM	7:24 AM	5:44 AM	8:06 AM	4:19 PM	4:55 PM	8:06 PM	3:55 PM

Prov=Providence; SF=San Francisco; Syd=Sydney; Lon=London
Times are presented in the standard time of the geographical location, using the current time zone of that place.

Window on the Weather

THE BEGINNING of solar cycle 25 promises renewal and hope to the planet, as is common at the beginning of an 11-year solar cycle. Given that the new cycle will likely be as weak as the last, a gradual cyclical cooling of the planet at mid latitudes is also a likely outcome for now. The recent increase in volcanic activity mimics similar periods from the past that resulted in cool Summers and fiercely cold Winters across the United States, Europe and the Pacific Rim Countries, with similar conditions during Southern Hemisphere Winters.

The majority of the instances of this pattern occurred during two periods of low solar activity and low sunspot count during the early modern period. From 1645–1715 the Maunder Minimum changed the economies of Europe during fiercely cold Winters. The Dalton Minimum from 1790–1830 resulted in cooling that drove settlers from New England to warmer southern climates. Modern agricultural practices have mitigated some of the economic risk. In the United States, the outlook is for crop abundance for at least the next five years, into the solar peak.

MARCH 2021 As the second year of solar cycle 25 begins, the Sun's ultraviolet output remains relatively weak, favoring late season snowfalls from the mid-Atlantic states north to New England and west through the Great Lakes. Such weather behavior highlights how efficient Nature is by providing nitrogen at precisely the time that the natural fertilizer can be useful for plant growth. A wetter than normal weather pattern likely persists throughout much of the South, from Dallas to Atlanta and through the Carolinas. Colder than normal weather is also likely farther north into New England. Weather systems usually advance slowly during Spring, with the current beginning of solar cycle 25 also slowing the pattern. A late season snowfall is also likely in Chicago. The West Coast remains stormy with wind-swept gales from Seattle to Portland early in the month. California enjoys generally sunny and mild weather.

APRIL 2021 Cold and damp weather persists along much of the Eastern Seaboard, with a late season snowstorm from interior New England to Upstate New York. Farther south an outbreak of severe weather will spawn tornadoes from Georgia to Mississippi by the 10th. Above normal Spring rainfall is also likely there and farther west through the Mississippi Valley. Such weather foretells a strong growing season, even as cold weather persists across the plains from Dallas north to Minneapolis through mid-month. Stormy weather eases along the West Coast, even as low clouds, fog and drizzle persist. A deep snow-pack persists across higher elevations of the inter-mountain West, lengthening the Winter sports season. Arizona enjoys beautiful Spring weather as does Southern California.

MAY 2021 During low points in 11-year solar cycles, general weather patterns and individual storms tend to move slowly. The severe weather risk shifts north during the month, with the greatest risk from the Central Plains to the Ohio Valley. Wet weather persists from Minneapolis eastward through the Great Lakes. The growing season is well underway south of those areas, with generally sunny days across the Mississippi Valley, throughout the Tennessee Valley and much of the Southeast. On occasion, the advance of cool air will cause thunderstorm outbreaks there, with gusty winds and brief, heavy rainfall. Unusually warm ocean water temperatures keep Florida abnormally hot and a brief tropical disturbance cannot be ruled out there. Beautiful Spring weather persists through the Rockies with warm days and chilly nights as mountain snowmelts increase.

JUNE 2021 In general, June weather will be spectacular this year, with fine growing conditions across the United States Heartland. Warm days and pleasantly cool nights will prevail across the Midwest, while above normal temperatures will persist along the East Coast. However, spells of cloudy and cool weather will develop from New York to Boston with several stretches of heavy rain and the possibility of flooding in the mountains farther north. The weather is especially fine across the Great Lakes, with daily temperatures averaging in the low 70s and night-time temperatures in the low 50s. West Coast weather is beautiful. A little fog lingers near the coast. Heat builds across the Southern Plains, including Dallas, but still no drought is indicated this year. Florida's temperatures remain above normal.

JULY 2021 Ideal growing conditions are leading to abundant crops this Summer. Above normal temperatures in the Southern Plains can stress yields there. Still, the overall outlook is positive this year with somewhat cooler than normal temperatures.

Should social trends persist concerning migration away from cities and to nature and outdoor enjoyment, this Summer will not be a disappointment across much of the country. At times northeastern U.S. cities will enjoy coastal sea breezes and morning fog. Several afternoons of strong thunderstorms are likely in New England. Temperatures will be most variable across the Great Lakes, where thunderstorms are likely. Afternoon thunderstorms are also probable in Florida's coastal communities and through the inter-mountain West. The West Coast enjoys pleasant Summer weather with harbor fog each afternoon from California to Washington State.

AUGUST 2021 Changes in sea surface temperature distribution across the Atlantic Ocean favor another year of increased hurricanes and an ongoing threat to the Gulf states and East Coast. Early season tropical disturbances are a great risk to Florida. Accompanying such activity, a channel of persistent rain is likely to emerge and bring drenching rains to much of the East Coast with flooding a risk for the Western Carolinas, North Georgia mountains and progressing north to New England throughout the month. August weather remains pleasant farther west with cool nights and warm days. Afternoons bring thunderstorms west of Denver and a Pacific hurricane brings rainfall east of Los Angeles.

SEPTEMBER 2021 Solar cycle theory implies that this will be the second of three active hurricane series, part of a natural cycle that thins out woodlands and provides conditions for ecological renewal. The chances are increased for one or more storms to make landfall along the East Coast of the United States. Across the Western U.S., equal and opposite conditions increase fire risk as part of a similar cycle. Unseasonably warm weather continues from the Ohio Valley eastward. Rainfall is heavy at times with persistent southerly winds. Monsoon-like rains are also present through the mountainous West, but get out your ski gear because an unusual mountain snowfall is likely in the Northern Rockies by the end of the month.

OCTOBER 2021 Although the hurricane risk diminishes rapidly during the month throughout most of the Eastern Seaboard, South Florida and the Gulf Coast are still somewhat vulnerable. Fall foliage lovers will be relieved that heavy rains ease farther north with a fine spell of Fall weather arriving in New England as the leaves change color. A Full Moon frost punctuates the end of the growing season across the Northern Plains and Pacific Northwest. Fires persist in parts of Southern California, while afternoon thunderstorms bring welcome mountain rains to Northern Arizona. Tropical east winds bring several days of downpours to Florida, where temperatures remain above normal. In general, crops are abundant this year.

NOVEMBER 2021 As solar cycle 25 continues to advance through its early stages, early Winters are likely, correlating with other such periods in history. Much of the cold weather will begin in the Northern Rockies where early snows are likely from Spokane, Washington to Denver. Early cold is also likely to emerge throughout the Northern Plains and snow squalls will arrive across Michigan with locally heavy accumulations after the 20th. The East Coast can expect a beautiful mid Fall, as the month will begin with pleasantly mild weather along the Eastern Seaboard with little rainfall. Southern heat will break as the first frosts arrive from the Carolinas to North Georgia around the 30th. Dry weather returns to Florida with warm days and cool nights. Fire remains a risk for Southern California, as dry and hot winds arrive from mountains near the coast.

DECEMBER 2021 Early season snows arrive through much of the Eastern and Central United States, a divergence from recent years which have been mild. The chances for snow is likely by Yule from Boston westward to Chicago. Persistent cold is also likely with a record chill possible in many places. Lake-effect snows bring severe Winter conditions from Buffalo to Syracuse and also the northeastern suburbs of Cleveland. Cold weather arrives early in Atlanta, as temperatures drop well below freezing at night by mid month. Gusty northwest winds increase the fire risk across Florida's Everglades.

In general, the West will be pleasantly mild and sunny. However, windswept gales will arrive in Seattle after the 15th with heavy mountain snows. California remains dry with gusty desert winds in the South that can sweep into Los Angeles.

JANUARY 2022 The early stage of solar cycle 25, now underway, is characterized by cooling water temperatures across the Pacific Ocean and warming within the tropical Atlantic. Such conditions are correlated with below normal Winter temperatures across North America and above normal snowfall. While the eastern two thirds of the U.S. will be frigid this year, an outlier will be Florida where warm and dry weather is probable. Snowfall far above normal is likely from the Ohio Valley to New England with a series of relatively weak storms providing persistent unsettled weather. An ice storm is a risk across the Mid-Atlantic. Snowfall is light and the air frigid in the Northern Rockies, while the West Coast is sunny and mild with areas of coastal fog.

FEBRUARY 2022 Nationally, February will be the snowiest month this year, with storms crossing the Rockies and blanketing a large swath of the nation from Denver eastward to New York City. Several coastal storms will focus over a foot of snow from Philadelphia to Boston. Farther south an outbreak or two of nighttime thunderstorms can produce isolated tornadoes from the Carolinas south through Georgia and Florida. The West Coast enjoys a break from dry weather with several days of rain turning hillsides green. Temperatures will turn cooler than normal with daily highs averaging in the 50s in San Francisco. Chicago endures one of the coldest Februaries on record.

✳ the fixed stars

Betelgeuse

"Betelgeuse is having a moment," said one stargazer during October of 2019. This comment was in response to an explosive celestial drama happening on the surface of Betelgeuse. The familiar star in the constellation Orion was the 10th brightest light in the night sky until it exploded. It has been gradually dimming ever since. The reddish orange super giant, which is about 950 times larger than our Sun, apparently is in the process of becoming a supernova. It is expected to expand in size and grow very bright before eventually cooling and shrinking into a dwarf. The last supernova event was first observed on February 23–24, in 1987. Before that it was Kepler's star, also a supernova, observed in 1604. There is no way to know whether Betelgeuse will explode again, expanding in size soon, or whether this will occur over a period of hundreds or even thousands of years. When it does happen though astronomers expect Betelgeuse to become even brighter than the Moon in our sky. It may even be bright enough to cast shadows during the daytime. Betelgeuse is pronounced Beetlejuice, just like the enigmatic ghoul character played by Michael Keaton in the 1988 Tim Burton film. Perhaps there is something in the name. Maybe the film offers some subtle messages, insights and synchronicities about the great red star.

Since Betelgeuse is thought to be about a trillion miles and approximately 640 light years away its heightened activity and transformation

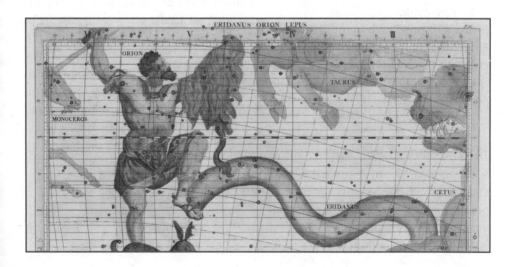

doesn't pose a physical threat to planet Earth. This distant sun is so bright though, it has intrigued sky watchers since ancient times. Betelgeuse is estimated to be about 10 million years old and thought to have actually began to gradually turn into a red supernova 40 thousand years ago or so. Astrology deals with how the subtle energies the planets and stellar bodies emit affect our quality of life in various ways.

The name Betelgeuse is actually derived from the Arabic and refers to the right shoulder of the constellation Orion. It sparkles above the club hand of the Great Hunter and is the brightest star in Orion. Once Betelgeuse finally disappears that constellation will be no more. Although changes in the skies above occur over many thousands of years, they are still very dynamic. Stars are distant suns, forever in motion, dying and being born. For example the Pleiades did not yet exist when the dinosaurs roamed the Earth. Astrologically all of this current excitement acts like something of an exclamation point, drawing attention to how this fixed star affects horoscope interpretation. Currently Betelgeuse is located at 28 degrees Gemini 53 minutes. A very small orb, a maximum of only three degrees, is suggested. This means that all of those born near the Summer Solstice, from June 17–22 of any year, will have Betelgeuse conjunct the natal Sun. In considering how the Moon and planets which might be affected check for chart placements from 25 degrees Gemini through 2 degrees of Cancer.

Ptolemy, a Greek mathematician and astrologer who originally catalogued many fixed stars, assigned Betelgeuse a Mercury-Mars influence. Here are keynotes for interpretation when Betelgeuse is conjoined by astrological bodies in individual horoscopes or event charts. Consider only the conjunction, not the other aspects, in fixed star interpretation.

With the Sun—command, military distinction, ability in mystical studies, tendency toward fevers

With the Moon—attracts honor and wealth, turbulent emotions, active mind

With Mercury—studious, literary, scientific, healthy, poor financial circumstances

With Venus—reserved, artistic talents, good finances, turmoil in family life

With Mars or Pluto—good organizer, military success, leadership ability

With Jupiter—studious, drawn to law or religion, shrewd and fortunate in business

With Saturn—clever but not always honest, eventful life with changeable luck

With Uranus—attracts dubious friends, mercurial and indecisive, self absorbed

With Neptune—mediumship ability, psychic, many journeys over water, a gambler

During the year ahead Mars will conjoin Betelgeuse from April 15 -April 27, 2021. The Full Moon on December 18, 2021 will be almost exactly conjunct Betelgeuse. These are excellent times to observe how this fixed star can relate to one's personal destiny as well as mirroring global situations.

–DIKKI-JO MULLEN

Getting to the Bones of Witchcraft

Looking in The Magic Mirror

WITCHES WITH Jewish backgrounds sometimes ignore Judaism in favor of pagan attitudes, but there is so much magic in Judaism that it is foolish to neglect it. The following discussion of Witchcraft arises from reflections on Judaism and Judaic magical heritage in conversation with other Witches.

The term here is Witchcraft, not magic. This is something wholly distinct and worth addressing. Language is something that allows for description rather than relying exclusively on hard definitions. To many, Witchcraft is a religion with a spirituality. While you can belong to a tradition that matches that description, this is not what Witchcraft is at its bones. That is not to denigrate traditions that add religious elements, only to point out that Witchcraft exists in many ways.

Talmud and Judaic Witchcraft

The Hebrew bible is full of magic and Paganism which is given deeper meaning in its rabbinical context found in the Talmud. The *Babylonian Talmud* has been called a spell book and that is not far from wrong. While Christians used the Hebrew bible to commit atrocities in the name of *Exodus* despite having the New Testament that could have tempered this, why didn't Jews do likewise? One of the main reasons is Talmud. The bible was never treated simply and was never meant to be—for Jews it is something worked with and interpreted.

In the Talmud there is one curse against Witches found in tractate *Pesachim*, and one story recounting that Rabbi Simeon ben Shetach executed a coven of eighty Witches in Ashkelon. It is a very sad story and it was not just the women who suffered, but the condemnation was not nearly as widespread as what we see in European Witch-hunts. The seventh chapter of the *Mishnah Sanhedrin* relates a story about rabbis discussing Witchcraft, and while they may disapprove, they are also aware that their wives engage in Witchcraft. This story seems to imply that this was an old pattern as well as something that clearly had to be tolerated to some degree. Folk magic changes to work within the dominating religion, such as seen in the spell of the cunning craft which employs Christian prayers to the Father, Son and Holy Ghost.

In Talmud the rabbis practice magic that is largely based around information, knowledge and spiritual work. Witchcraft is something more organic and the two can blur. While Witches can be men of course, it's a current that flows mostly from women. Sexism has caused some

disapproval of Witchcraft from men. However there are places where men are more associated with Witchcraft, so this is debatable and may vary regionally. The famous Rabbi Rashi had a daughter who practiced magic. It was said she was powerful and could work the magic of men and women. This implies that LGBTQ people have a potent place in magic because they can bridge these forces.

The Judaic elements of Witchcraft appear to come in two forms, folk magic and poisoning. Folk magic is used in common ways for common things, to protect and heal and find love as well as counter magic. Some might split these two up as many counter magical traditions specifically oppose Witchcraft, but Witches also perform counter magic. Poisoning does not just refer to actual poisons, though they are included, but malicious Witchcraft. Value judgements and morality aside, it is something that is practiced.

There was an element to Witchcraft that was generally beneficial or that was expected to go on which the rabbis of the Talmud ignored, such as healing. Then there was magic to harm, mostly

out of malice and vengeance, and although the rabbis rarely discovered or punished it, this is where society would take issue.

This is a common pattern outside Judaism. As a quick example, the word in ancient Greek for Witchcraft was *pharmakeia* (medicine, drugs, spells), and was distinct from *magos* (magician) and *goes* (sorcerer). It is of course where we get our modern word pharmacy due to its use and common associations with drugs, herbs and poisons. Witchcraft was an illicit religion of sorts and was an ancient power. Even the gods could be affected by this power. Ancient Greek and Judaic practices are separate, but this shows how distinct such practices can be and how language shows this.

Following the thread

Few people practicing magic just use one form of magic, some magi-cians will work with Witchcraft, and plenty of Witches take a formal occult approach. In magic these things bridge and blur, but at times the point is to not blend. In terms of simply distinguishing Witchcraft from magic, you may agree and understand this, though words will largely fail to do the meaning justice. Witchcraft does not need books and information—certainly they can help—but ultimately it comes from people, the environment, and yourself.

People is your place in your community, with your family and those you meet. Magic passes between people physically as well as through presence, states of mind, conversation and engagement with people. The environment is our relationship with the land, and on a regional level this can get interesting. It's why magic

changes by region and yet there are common threads. Yourself is the Witchcraft within you, that works in your blood, mind and bone. How you live and how you treat yourself and everything around you influences your relationship to it.

Academia allows us to speak about a branch of magic that is largely unspoken. Witchcraft is the magic that people often do not think of as magic, that is part of everyday life and resources, and is also something between and beyond the hedge, eldritch and otherworldly, yet familiar. Witchcraft is also stories of women meeting in the evening, sitting on the porch with bottles of wine and getting out the tarot cards. There are practitioners who eagerly try and find out more of the unspoken magic of their cultures, but who would not want to share that publicly.

At its core Witchcraft is of the heart and blood and not something that happens in a cerebral way, yet the mind can be a tool in time. Witchcraft expresses itself in your ability to converse within yourself and the world around you, letting the plants tell you the magic they can work with you to do, the powers of others combining with your own, how the spirits around you will gift you in exchange for service or simply conversation or friendship and gifts of your own. The spirituality or traditions that come from this, and really all magic, are byproducts and helpful ways to develop a working vocabulary. They can also mean we lose the foundations beneath the structure and striking a balance can be hard.

Witchcraft is the union of instinct, imagination, thought, intent and environment.

An easy way to see this is how you engage with the power of plants around you. Some speak the language of plants naturally as an innate power, while some learn this as a developed power, but how plants grow and look will tell you their powers. They will call to your blood how they can work magic with you. You find you do not need to be an herbalist because the magic is there, equally you can be a herbalist and it will compliment your craft, but this comes from conversation and how your instincts guide you in correlation with the land you are on.

Get some drinks, tarot cards and candles and meet with friends and see what happens next, what magic is produced from your conversation and your laughter echoing into the night.

—RICHARD LEVY

Dice or no Dice?

AT VINTAGE CAR shows the hot rods, the muscle cars of the 1940s through the 1960s, offer onlookers a silent statement. A quick glance tells it all. The clue is dangling from the rear-view mirrors in the ubiquitous form of the eye catching, soft and fuzzy, plush, oversized dice in bright colors. Adventure, fun, speed and a belief in luck all come to mind with a glimpse of the dice. Fuzzy dice first appeared during World War II when fighter pilots hung them above their instrument panels as good luck symbols when facing risky missions.

At Leu Gardens in Orlando, Florida in the Spring of 2020 a sculpture of bright red dice approximately eight feet high was featured in a display of outdoor games as an introduction and photo op. Visitors posed with the giant dice for picture taking just as the era of social distancing and the coronavirus was beginning; hopefully they were able to capture a moment of humor and good luck to carry them through the dark times ahead.

Dice have been popular for thousands of years. These small handheld objects appear all around the globe. They are tossed to determine the outcome of gambles in games and for divination, to offer insight into human destiny.

Dice (or singular die) are most commonly cubic with six sides. Indented or painted dots also called pips give each side a number, usually from one to six. They are truly random though only when precision made with the dots flush with the sides. When the markings are indented, slight variations in weight occur. This can affect the outcome of the toss.

Dice can be polyhedrons made with eight, ten, twelve, twenty or even more sides. Sometimes pictures or other symbols will replace the familiar pips. Astrologers might use astro-dice, marked with symbols for the Zodiac signs, the Sun, Moon, planets and numerals indicating the houses of the Zodiac. This invokes an element of chance to offer an esoteric look at reading horoscopes and interpreting the outcome of celestial transits.

Knuckle bones created from small animal bones have been found around the world in prehistoric sites. These suggest dice-like games dating back to the stone age. In the ruins of Ur, a city in ancient Mesopotamia, a board game was found which used four-sided pyramidal dice. Around 3000 B.C.E. the Egyptians played a table top game called Senet with dice-like objects. In Iran, dating from about 2500 B.C.E., early dice sets were found which appear to have been part of a backgammon-like game. Sophocles claimed in the fifth century B.C.E. that dice were invented by the Greeks during the siege of Troy. Dice appeared in China by 600 B.C.E. References to "casting lots" in the Bible also describe the use of dice-like objects to determine choices. Marco Polo is thought to have brought dice sets back from Asia to Italy during the late 13th century.

The word dice actually comes from the Old French word *deh* [dice]. This is derived from the Latin word *datum*, meaning something played or given. Dice are and have long been everywhere. Across the ages the charm of dice continues to attract and intrigue people. Today they are used in a variety of games and for divination, much as dominos are. Dice convey meaning when referenced in everyday conversations. Saying, "no dice" means a situation is at a dead end, that it isn't working out. "It's a roll of the dice," means something might go either way. Fate is at work and the outcome is a matter of luck. "Weighted dice," warns of unfairness and dishonest dealings at work, while just saying "dice" is encouraging. A desirable outcome is assured.

—ELAINE NEUMEIER

Clear Crystal Quartz

The King of Crystals

Called the king of crystals, quartz is all purpose and pure as ice. The common occurrence of quartz led to the variety of myths and historic folk practices that surround it, and it is still a powerful ally.

King of the Mineral Realm

Quartz shows up in the lore of ancient Rome, Japan, Australia, Egypt and in Native American cultures. One Cherokee myth tells of how quartz crystal became the master healer, the king of all crystals.

CRYSTALS are a potent source of magical energy. When many people hear the term crystal they immediately think of the prisms hung from windows that create rainbows when spun. Others think of hippies and mystical new agers looking for inner peace and a heightened awareness of their spiritual bodies. These associations are tied to one of the most common crystals in the planet's crust: quartz. It is the most versatile crystal in magic, able to be used for almost any purpose. It is referenced as an important ally in folklore across the world. From healing to calling rain, protecting cattle to connecting with spirits, quartz crystals have a long list of magical and spiritual properties.

Historically, magicians could only work with materials they could obtain locally or through trade. They were limited in the crystals of their choice, yet still made the most of what was available for them. Even though today you can order any crystal you can dream of online, the one you can still find anywhere is quartz.

There was a time when mankind was in tune with the land. Humans were thankful and respectful to everything that existed. But over time, people began to forget to say their prayers and be thankful to the spirits of the plants and animals that gave their life for human survival. When this began to happen, the animal, plant, insect and mineral tribes all met together. The animals decided to punish humans by making them sick if their meat is not properly prepared. The insects agreed to carry diseases that would be transmitted through their bites.

The plant kingdom took pity on humans and agreed that while some of them would make humans sick, the rest would be used as medicine, except for tobacco which was the king of the plants. This they decided would be the sacred herb and bring blessings and prayers from the humans to the gods, but if not respected it would bring the most serious of illnesses: cancer.

The quartz who was the king of the crystal tribe took pity on humans. Quartz decreed that each crystal and mineral would have its own vibration and power to heal the mind, body and spirit of humans, bringing them back to balance. As for itself, quartz declared that it would be the sacred mineral. Quartz believed that it was important to hold on to the record of this meeting and all other spiritual work, so it took on the ability to store and record history.

Thus clear quartz gained the ability to provide humans with spiritual messages when they gaze upon the crystal.

Ice and purity

The word crystal can be traced to the Greek word krystallos, meaning ice. The Roman natural historian and philosopher Pliny the Elder believed that quartz crystals were ice crystals or water that had been frozen so thoroughly that it could never thaw. One of the ways ancient cultures used the crystal was to carve it into rings and spheres that people could carry around with them in the summer to keep cool.

Dragons are traditionally associated with hoards of gold and treasure, and quartz crystal has its own associations with dragons. In Japanese lore, it is regarded as the perfect jewel—a symbol of perfection and the pursuit of perfection. This comes from one of the creation legends of Japan, in which quartz was created by the breath of a revered white dragon. This association

with perfection is one of the reasons quartz crystal is included in Japanese temple decorations.

Crystal balls and crystal skulls

As well as being a perfect gem, quartz found a place of importance within Tibetan Buddhism. Tibetan monks call quartz crystal balls "windows of the gods." Monks gaze upon crystals in meditation as symbols of the duality between the physical world and the spiritual ones. They believe that by gazing into the clarity of the crystal their thoughts become crystalized and so they are able to meditate and work towards attaining enlightenment.

Crystal gazing is also a practice associated with psychics, magicians, Witches and spirit workers. The stereotypical crystal ball for scrying originated as quartz crystals carved into spheres. By gazing upon the crystal and staring into the impurities—cracks and bubbles—and at the reflection of a flickering candle, one can contact spirits and work divination through the practice of scrying.

In the Britisth Museum, there are skulls carved from crystal that were originally supposed to be of Aztec or Mayan origin. Skulls are a common theme in Mesoamerican art, so when these beautiful and lurid crystals hit the market, museums and private collectors were eager to buy them. However, recent research has demonstrated that they are fakes, produced in the middle of the 20th century. The original tale was that the crystal skulls were objects of power found in caves. The shape supposedly indicated that their long dead crafters believed their ancestors lived within the crystals or at least that the crystals provided communication between the faithful and their ancestors . It's a good story—too bad it isn't true! But imitations of these objects are common in pagan shops, and modern people wishing to offer reverence and prayer to ancestors can nonetheless use them for this purpose. What started as a sales pitch has transformed into a beautiful concept of practice for those who embrace the whole cycle of human life and death.

Health, wellness and healing

In ancient Egypt the power of quartz was well known. Egyptian artisans carved drinking vessels out of quartz. These crystals absorb the power and vitality of the Sun , so by drinking out a glass carved from crystal, the water becomes imbued with the power of the crystal, allowing the transfer of power to go from sun to crystal to water to human.

The ancient Greeks and Romans knew that they could use quartz to heal. Like the Egyptians, they took advantage of the solar properties of the crystal for their healing work. Doctors used the crystal as a lens to focus light and cauterize wounds. The crystals were also used to light many sacred fires, including the fires of the Eleusinian Mysteries.

Healing is the most common practice associated with quartz crystals, and appears in many variations across the world. There is a Celtic method for using quartz to maintain and restore health:

Place nine quartz crystals in a pot and fill it with water.

Boil the water and let it cool.

Drink the water over the next nine days.

The reputation for quartz as an all-purpose crystal and is more than earned. The versatility in both ancient and modern practices shows that quartz really can be used for anything you can imagine. It is clear, pure and perfect for magical work. Call it clear quartz rock, ice crystal or quartz. Use it as a mirror or for scrying. No matter how you relate to it, let the crystal guide you on your journey. May you unlock the mysteries of the crystal by gazing into its depths!

—LOONA WYND

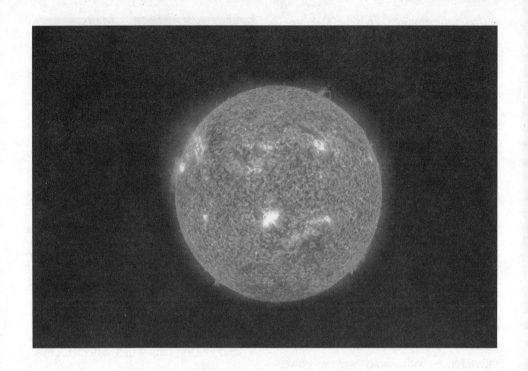

Sunspots, Starspots

*Solar Flares, Winds, Coronal Loops, Prominences, Mass Ejections,
Reconnection Events and Storms.*

WE ARE sunlight. The Sun provides Earth, our home, with the energy which makes all life possible. Astrologically the Sun sign in the birth chart is the familiar Zodiac sign everyone knows. It is planet Earth's path around the Sun on the date of birth. The Sun sign in the horoscope reveals where and how one can shine in life. However, this glowing golden sphere also keeps some secrets. It has wicked, mysterious and playful sides.

Exploring the phenomenon of sunspots is a good way to begin to understand more about what the Sun really is. Although Galileo (1564–1642) has often been given credit for discovering sunspots,

the earliest reports about them actually date back much further, beginning about 800 B.C.E. with the Chinese *Book of Changes*. Near 300 B.C.E. the Greek scholar Theophrastus, who studied with Plato, left recordings of careful, deliberate sunspot observation. John, also known as Florence, of Worcester was an English monk and historian who drew pictures of sunspots in December 1128 C.E..

The larger spots can be seen with the naked eye. Some can be many times larger than planet Earth. Sunspots are darker areas which, although still very hot, are somewhat cooler (about 2,700 degrees Celsius) than the Sun's overall surface temperature (about 5,500 degrees Celsius.) Usually sunspots develop in pairs of opposite magnetic polarity. Fluctuations in convection are what cause spots to form. They expand and contract while traveling across the Sun's surface. Eventually they will decay and disappear, after a few days or a couple of months. The numbers of sunspots varies from none at all sometimes to many at other times. They follow cycles of approximately 11 years with some variations in length.

The impact of sunspot activity on Earth is a hotly debated topic in scientific circles. Some astronomers insist that they have no affect at all, while others will link sunspots to temperature fluctuations, earthquakes, various disturbed weather patterns, the growth of tree rings, interference with radio waves, power outages, wars, migrations, illnesses, crusades, revolutions and other significant earthly events.

Over the past 400 years studies of sunspot cycles have led to separating them into maxima and minima trends, as the number rises and falls, respectively. During the early to mid 20th century the trend was upwards, which many scientists felt corelated with a cooling temperature trend. More recently sunspot activity has tapered off, possibly indicating warmer temperatures. Overall, though, the Sun's activity is accelerating. Most scientists agree that current solar radiation is more dynamic than it has been in the past eight thousand years.

The story of sunspots doesn't stop here, though. They are accompanied by and appear to cause a great deal of secondary intense magnetic activity which also can be linked to earthly events:

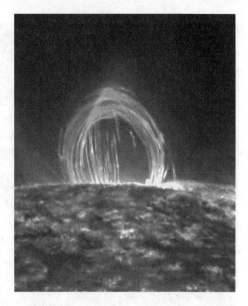

- Solar flares are especially high energy emissions. The solar flares send out protons which affect Earth's atmosphere.
- Powerful auroras can appear as the Northern and Southern Lights upon interacting with Earth's magnetic field.
- Solar winds are streams of charged particles released from the Sun's upper atmosphere. The wind is a plasma consisting of electrons, protons and alpha particles charged with kinetic energy.
- Coronal loops are huge energy circles which begin and end on the Sun's surface.
- A mass ejection is a giant cloud of solar plasma drenched with lines of a magnetic field as it is blown away from the Sun.
- A solar prominence is a large, bright, gaseous feature extending outward from the Sun's surface, often shaped in a loop. This anchors to the Sun's surface and extends outward to the Sun's corona. The corona, from the

Latin word for crown, is a ring of plasma surrounding the Sun.

- Solar storms are events in which activity induced by radiation and streams of charged particles on the Sun interferes with Earth's magnetic field. Because the Sun is so far away, many people believe that these storms are not capable of having any impact. However they seem to occur along with events which are quite significant, even devastating.
- A solar reconnection event is a process in which magnetic field lines are spliced to one another. These patterns of connectivity are changeable and dynamic.

The study of sunspots unlocks a deeper understanding of the complex patterns of action at work within the Sun. With advances in technology, more and more is being discovered all the time about the Sun, Earth's celestial life light. Of course this has all been happening for millions of years; however, as humanity becomes capable of discovering more about the Sun, perhaps humans are growing more sophisticated in the ability to respond to a wider range of its amazing energies.

The countless stars visible in the night sky after sunset are also distant suns, and many also have spots. These stellar phenomena are called starspots. Most stars are so far away that detectable fluctuations in brightness are hard to discern. However, among those which can be observed starspots are often impressive. Astronomical calculations suggest that some starspots might be 100 times larger than those on the Sun and cover over 30 percent of the star's surface.

Spaceplace.Nasa.gov/solaractivity is a good link for further information about the Sun. Daily updates are readily available with reports about current sunspot and other solar activity. Never gaze directly at the Sun, as that can cause permanent damage to the eyes. Check with a local planetarium or observatory for more information and for help in safely observing sunspots.

—DIKKI-JO MULLEN

A Gentle Nudge or
a Thunderbolt?

WHEN YOU really want something or someone, it is very tempting to make it happen magically. The seventies and eighties were very interesting times! Being able to influence outcomes through magic was quite heady.

Elizabeth Pepper and Lord Theo Mills were nurturing spiritual parents. Both were extremely adept magicians and excellent teachers and mentors. Teddy's approach was more along the line of fire and fury, whereas Elizabeth had a gentler touch. Elizabeth was a natural life coach. She was nonjudgmental, a good listener and an easy conversationalist. She was very powerful in a quiet sort of way. The home she shared with her artist husband, Martin, was painted entirely in primary colors, including the floors. Warm oriental carpets covered the floors, and rug covered ledges for their umpteen cats adorned the walls. It was a joyful place to visit, and her garden full of herbs was a delight. In her gracious company you always felt cared for and loved. Walks and talks with her were always an inspiration.

Teddy lived in a small dark apartment that was full of magic, and he did love to show off. Ted used to love to create storms, over just one house for example. Creating weather was his specialty. He enjoyed putting on a show and performed many magical feats. Some were fun and others were pretty scary. Many of the local constabulary thoroughly enjoyed his shenanigans and came to him for help and tarot readings. Ted was an excellent reader, and he relished manipulating people and things. He was also generous, but you did not want to cross him.

Lord Theo was very careful to keep students who lacked fortitude and were too sensitive away from highly charged negative experiences, dark energies and exorcisms. This made some who wanted to be helpful feel left out, but in the long run was a wise choice because they probably would not have fared well. It was not difficult to notice a gradual waning of life force from the huge amount of energy these clearings took. It was challenging for Teddy and for those who helped him to recover from treacherous endeavors that helped people in need.

It is tempting to use magic to manipulate people and events to get what

100

you want. Magic can be very effective, and when done in the right frame of mind is an able tool and friend. It can also backfire on you, for example in romance. Pretty much everyone wants a fulfilling relationship, and when you are strongly attracted to someone and know they are the person for you, naturally you want to do everything you can to make a connection happen.

Teddy used to tell a story about a woman he found very attractive. He wanted her to have the same feelings for him, so he decided to do a spell that had something to do with 49 petals. It worked and he got his love, but after some time he began to have regrets as the relationship wasn't turning out the way he thought it would. Unfortunately, he couldn't get rid of her, and he definitely regretted doing that ritual. He didn't regret it enough to stop manipulating people and situations, but he became much more cautious.

The totality of why individuals choose to incarnate into the lives they have, and what experiences are meant to be on their paths is a mystery. By manipulating and forcing, you may not be allowing the best person, job, housing et cetera to show up, or you may be so focused on what you want that you can't even see it. You may miss out on experiences that are meant for you to grow, and are part of your life path. That is not to say don't do ritual to influence outcomes. If doing spell work feels right to you, do it in a way that allows for something new, that perhaps you hadn't even thought of to show up. If it suits your magic, keep your desires open minded and your commands open

ended. Karma can be a bitch and bite you in the ass pretty fast. It may not be in another life.

Timing is everything. Sometimes the person or situation you are seeking hasn't shown up yet, or you have more growing to do to match the other person. There is nothing wrong with asking for things to speed up! However, trust that you are experiencing the results of the choices you are making and what is right for you in the moment. You can change what you don't like in your life. It just may be that what you really need to change is yourself.

Doing your best to live in the frequency of love 24 hours a day, getting out of your own way, being the gift, love and oneness of Source, God, or Goddess and walking your talk is the most magical way to live. You can try to force things, which creates stress and tension, or you can live in the flow and be open to possibilities, which is a more allowing and peaceful way to be in a human body, with all the challenges that entails!

—JANEAN STRONG

A VOICE FROM THE HEAVENS

Ancestor Veneration and the Egungun Masquerade

THE YORUBA of Southwest Nigeria and Benin would think it unconscionable to begin their day without the proper propitiation of the Ancestors. In fact, of the various spirits—the Gods, nature and the Ancestors—it is the Ancestors that are first to be addressed during morning prayers and are considered to be the closest to the living. The Ancestors are a vital part of the cosmological order of the universe. In fact, to the Yoruba, a family is made up of both the living and the deceased and each must be cared for in order for the family to be whole and prosperous. To that end, it is only after a good conversation as well as the proper offerings—water, morning beverage and kola nuts—are given to the Ancestors is

it proper to approach the divinities. It is the Ancestors who provide a temporal link to the past as well as serving as a link between the world of the living and the world of spirits.

The familial relationship between the living and their ancestors assures that there will always be a mutually beneficial relationship. For the Yoruba, the relationship between a father and child (or any elder and younger relative for that matter) does not cease with the death of the elder. In life, the relationship between an elder and a younger relative is one wherein the elder provides a guiding hand and gentle advice to the younger. Younger relations expect that elders will guide them to making good and sustainable decisions. The death of an elder does not sever that relationship. In fact the elder assumes the role of guiding ancestor in addition to assuming the new role of spirit intermediary. The relationship is one that is now necessarily changed and, in more ways than one, is now elevated.

The Death of an Elder

The family is assured a good relationship with the departed elder firstly by meticulously attending to the traditions of burial. These traditions vary not only from family to family but also by region to region. That being said, there are traditions that are universal among the Yoruba. In fact, some of these traditions are adhered to even by families that are Christian or Moslem.

On the death of an elder, the body is immediately wrapped in a mat and the family sends out the message of the crossing over. The single most important act of the funerary customs is the washing of the body of the deceased. In the case of the death of a male, the eldest son would be summoned home if he had moved away. He must be present when the body is washed, in fact it would be he who would pour the first of the water over the body. In the case of men, the head of the deceased is often shaved. Care would be taken if the deceased had in life been initiated into the cult of any of the Orisha (deities). In this case the lead priest of the cult or his charge be summoned, and they would take care of the proper treatment of the deceased's head, as this was the seat of the Orisha for initiation. In the case

of women, their hair is usually plaited in the fashion of the family or of the Orisha if they were initiated.

Once washed and shaved, the body would be attired in festive clothing and laid out on a freshly made and decorated bed. The family would invite the extended family and friends to the home to celebrate the life of the newly passed elder. For the most part, these celebrations could last a number of days. Each successive day would bring a new bath and a change of clothing. It was anticipated that each change of clothing would progressively become more refined, so that on the last day they would be wearing their finest. There would be much drumming and feasting and storytelling. As the elder becomes an Ancestor, the family celebrates their life and their deeds.

In times past, the deceased would have been buried in the living room of the house, digging down in the earth until red clay was reached (usually

family matters. It is expected that the ancestors will watch over the family, while the family will make sure to elevate the souls of the ancestors by means of remembering them through offerings on a daily basis as well as through annual celebration of the Egungun festival.

The Mask and the Masquerade

The Egungun (translating as masquerade) is a secret society of the Yoruba, whose sole function is to act as representatives of the collective ancestry of a given area. They commemorate the ancestors of a given area annually through a festival where masks representing the collective ancestors as well as individual deceased are donned and paraded/danced through town in June before the farming of yam.

around six feet). In this way it was felt that the Ancestor could participate in the daily life of the family. This custom has ceased in the modern era of poured foundations. Most Yoruba live in small family compounds that contain a few homes for extended family. The compound would also have a small area where the ancestors are buried. The final day would see the greatest feast of all culminating in the burial rites as the sun sets. The freshly dug grave would receive sacrifice, then the body which would be covered with a mat. The family places the elder's favorite daily items with the body in the grave. In the case of women this might include some of their jewelry, and in the case of men it might include hunting guns or the like.

The internment of the deceased does not end their participation in

The final task of the living done in the name of a deceased elder is the commission of a carving of a mask of the deceased for the annual festival of the Egungun society. This would not be done for every single ancestor—rather it is reserved for the most important and is usually done after an oracle has been consulted wherein the living are advised to make an Egungun mask of the elder. This is done by priest artisans who know the conventions of masks and know the medicine used in the fabrication of the costume that must accompany the mask. This mask would be presented to the chief priest of the local Egungun society and he would in turn secretly assign a priest who would wear the mask during the masquerade.

The masquerade of the Egungun is comprised of masks that represent specific individuals who have passed. In fact, each mask at one point represented a particular ancestor of the community. In reality, some of the masks have existed so long that they ceased to have a particular individual associated with them and have come to represent the pan-communal ancestors that are without name yet are elder to all in the community. The various types of mask are:

Agba Egungun These are the senior or elder masquerade and are the most important of the ritual masquerades. This grouping is the community ancestral. When a festival goer is approached by one of these masquerades, they would immediately remove any head covering and do a proper prostration before them. It is this class of masquerade that perform the holy rites in the sacred grove of the Egungun.

Alabebe These masqueraders follow the Agba in the festival. Their costumes are the most colorful of the masquerade.

They are usually followed by a retinue of women and children who will chant traditional praise poetry.

Paakara These masqueraders roam about singly rather than as part of a larger group. Their costumes might seem less abstract than most, being made up of shirt and trousers, with their heads being covered by a stocking with human like features painted on the front.

Alarinjo and Onidan These are masqueraders that can appear at any time of the year. These are more of entertainment than they are spiritual masquerades. The Onidan are known to perform tricks for spectators.

Agbegijo These are the masqueraders that have wooden headpieces and would for the most part be representative of specific individuals within the community.

The Annual Egungun Festival

Each year, the Yoruba honor the annual return of the ancestors to the world of

the living. The festival of the Egungun is tied to the agrarian calendar—the yam harvesting season that will dictate when the Egungun festival will be held. It is a not so subtle reminder to the living that death brings life and blessings; it is the ancestors who taught the living to farm the land.

The lead up to the actual festival precipitates a large amount of preparation activity, mundane as well as spiritual, that must be performed for a successful masquerade. While the ancestors are not considered divinity, the collective ancestry of a people are certainly elevated more than a particular individual might be. So much so that the Egungun, while considered a secret society, are also a priesthood much as one would encounter with any one of the Orisha.

Before the annual entry into the Egungun grove, each of the masquerades must have their medicine revitalized through chant, song and sacrifices. This would be the case not just for the Agba Egungun, but even the lesser masquerade. While the Alagba (chief priest) would attend to the Agba Egungun, the secondary priests would attend to the lesser Egungun masquerades.

The structure of the Egungun priesthood of a given geographic area is comprised completely of men save a single female, a priestess of Oya. Her inclusion as a chief within the society represents a recognition of Oya as being the mother of the Egungun. While women do not form the backbone of the Egungun priesthood, their participation in the annual festival is absolutely essential. It is the women who remember the praise poetry, familial lineages and songs that entreat the Ancestors to take possession of a masquerade to deliver messages to specific families.

During the festival, the Ancestors having mounted (possessed) the masquerade will carry messages to the individuals participating in the festival. In addition to very personal messages, non-priestly festival participants may seek answers from the mounted masquerade. Women who are trying to conceive will often ask the masquerade for help or to grant them children. Young men in search of a wife may also be found querying the masquerade as to what is required to secure an appropriated spouse. Because the Egungun expect the highest of standards, it would not be unusual for the Ancestor to chastise a querent for immorality. They will advise what behavior must be corrected as well as dictating what offerings must be made to atone for the bad behavior.

Outside of the annual Egungun Festival, there may be times where it is necessary for the masquerades to come out. This may be the result of a consultation with the oracles Ifa or Orisa. In this case, the retinue masquerade is smaller but still very public. Specific masquerades may be dictated by the oracle, along with an aggrieved ancestor that needs appeasement. In all cases, the appearance of the Egungun in the streets of towns and villages inspires a certain amount of fear, but it also assures the people of their continued guidance.

Honoring the Ancestors today

One does not need to be a priest or a masquerade to honor their Ancestors. Remembering our dead is the right of all living and would only serve to strengthen a family. You do not need to have access to the grave of the Ancestor. In fact, honoring them should take place in the home. The method should be your own, but should include the following:

- A remembrance and enumeration of the qualities of the Ancestor.
- Offerings that would be pleasing to the Ancestor—for example, if the Ancestor especially liked coffee, then coffee would be included in the offering.
- A method to verify that the offerings are acceptable—a simply binary yes–no system will do.

We all stand on the shoulders of those who have gone before us. Remembering your dead is not only for the dead—it is also for the living. It is a means of preserving your family and culture.

−IFADOYIN SANGOMUYIWA

The Ankh

ANCIENT EGYPTIANS believed that life was meaningful whether it was an earthly life or life in the hereafter. It is for this reason that their symbol for life figured so prominently in daily life as well as the funerary texts found on the walls of ancient burial chambers. Deities such as Isis or Anubis are often depicted pressing the ankh against the lips of the dead, allowing them to come to life in the underworld.

The prevalence of *wedjau*, as amulets were known to the Egyptians, pointed to the belief that supernatural benefits could be gained from their various charms. The ankh was one of three amulets that were commonly worn by Egyptians, the others being the *Wadjet* or the Eye of Horus for good health and the Djed or the Pillar for stability.

A simple symbol, the ankh is rich with meaning. It represents both the male and female genitalia, as well as a key to the gates of the afterlife. Its primary meaning of life can be found in the simple design, with the oval at the top representing the rising Sun, the cross bar representing the horizon over which the sun must climb and the path of the Sun through the underworld represented in the vertical bar.

The ankh reminds us that life is a continual cycle through which we pass. We can find hope in the rising sun, whether that be here on the physical plane or in the realms beyond.

—DEVON STRONG

Rethinking the Cup and the Knife

Decoupling Gender from the Practice of Witchcraft

FROM THE COSMOLOGY and theology of modern Witch traditions to the tools on the altar, the gendered language of Witchcraft is unavoidable. After all, how many modern Witches work with a Goddess and a God, or a Witchmother and Witchfather? What are the genders ascribed to the wand and the knife, or the cup and the paten? When practitioners envision a cauldron, who tends its fire and stirs its contents? Who is the Man in Black and who the Witch-Queen?

For many Witches, this gendering of the Craft is unremarkable, even natural. For them, Witchcraft operates in the context of a universe bound and maintained by the magical force of polarity, which they see as intrinsically, binarily gendered. They have no issues seeing the cauldron as the womb of their Goddess, or the union of the cup and the knife as a symbolic reenactment of the sexual union of gendered deities. Such Witches might even suggest that anyone out of sync with those cisgendered, heteronormative metaphors would find a more welcoming home elsewhere, away from what they see as the essential—and essentially gendered—mysteries of Witchcraft.

It's fair to note that this view is in every way traditional, in the sense of being a view held and promulgated by many like minded Witches over time. Likewise, it is not dismissive or disrespectful to suggest that it is also an artificially constrained view of what Witchcraft is and can be. This view, traditional though it might be, often fails to account either for the lived experiences of many Witches or for modern scientific understandings of biology, gender, and sexuality.

Of course, many of the devotional and spiritual practices of modern practitioners of Witchcraft are rooted in the past. In some cases, those practices are reconstructions or recreations of what practitioners believe their forebears did, while in other cases, they're an unabashed synthesis of ancient beliefs and ideas with modern techniques, perspectives and gnosis. In either case, Witches can find themselves struggling with the tension between the past and the present, between their own modern sensibilities and the realities of who their predecessors were and what they believed. That struggle is in no way ameliorated by modernity's unavoidably incomplete understanding of the past, which is as often informed by romantic fictions or idealized misinterpretations as by the historical record. What is a well-intentioned practitioner to do?

As L. P. Hartley wrote in The Go-Between, "The past is a foreign country: they do things differently there." Modern Witches aren't obligated to do as the ancients and ancestors did, nor even to believe what their ancestors did was good. However, they ought to be honest about who those ancestors were and what they did, to the best of their ability. They must be willing to look into their own practices and beliefs, and the cultures from which they derive, uncolored by a desire to

idealize the past or mold it to match modern expectations. This research can lead in unexpected directions, challenging both the researcher's own preconceptions and, in some cases, the very foundations of modern traditions of devotion and practice. With that in mind, Witches would do well to look at the metaphorical language woven through their own Craft, especially in relation to gender.

To focus on just a single example of modern Witch praxis, albeit perhaps the most commonly known rite in all of Witchcraft, many streams of modern Witchcraft employ a ritual variously known as the symbolic Great Rite, the Hieros Gamos (sacred marriage,) the consecration of the wine, and other names. In this rite, a pair of consecrated tools, the knife and the cup, are brought together in a fashion often interpreted as symbolizing heterosexual intercourse. One Witch, generally female, will hold the cup, and another Witch, generally male, will insert the knife into the cup. Variations exist where the genders are swapped, or a single Witch holds both cup and knife, but that's the basic frame. A great deal of theology has been spun from the metaphorical associations between the knife and the penis, the cup and the vagina, and the union of these tools with the union of whichever polar opposites the theologian values: male and female, light and dark, active and passive, and so on.

Again, this analysis is perfectly traditional and utterly valid. It is, however, incomplete and quite possibly a deviation from the initial and significantly deeper meaning of the symbology in this rite.

For an explanation, interested Witches are directed to the work of Empedocles, a pre-Socratic Greek philosopher of the 5th century BCE. While not among the A-list of Greek philosophers, Empedocles is highly relevant to modern Witches, Pagans and magical practitioners. He proposed the philosophical framing of the material universe as being composed of four roots, or elements: Earth, Air, Fire and Water. In his cosmological schema, the universe is formed of the union and separation of these four elements by two divine forces: *philotes* (love), which brings them together, and *neikos* (strife), which tears them apart. Where love rules all the condition of *harmonia* (harmony) prevail, while the rulership of strife creates the conditions of *khaos* (chaos.) It is from the interaction, the union of these forces, that worlds are born and life itself comes into being.

For Witches looking for a symbol to represent love, it would be hard to do better than the chalice, the loving cup,

the tool of harmony. Similarly, Witches seeking a symbol for strife need only reach for the knife, the athame, the weapon of the Witch. Truly, what better symbol could there be for the union of love and strife—the union which generates the universe itself—than that of the cup and the knife conjoined?

Perhaps ironically, Empedocles' schema reintroduces polarity, not as a gendered binary, but as a truly cosmic and all-encompassing principle. This isn't to say that viewing the union of cup and knife solely as a symbolic heterosexual sacred marriage is wrong or invalid, merely that it's limited and limiting. After all, love and strife are the primal divine forces of creation and destruction, which are hardly unique to any gender, female or male or otherwise. Affixing to these powers any mortal notions of gender, or indeed any other cultural norms, seems little more than an attempt to constrain those powers within a tidy schema which suits one's preconceived notions. Conversely, the act of decoupling gender from the symbols in play removes those limitations and reveals a profound depth and complexity of meaning and magical power within them. It frees the Witch to explore the inner meanings of the rite, and unfolds an entire new world of spiritual and magical resonances.

With so much magic to be found beneath the surface of just this one rite, modern Witches are invited to consider how much more could be divined throughout their Craft, merely by letting go of the language of gender and opening themselves to the possibility of a deeper magic.

—Misha Magdalene

EVERYDAY KITCHEN

WITCHERY

KITCHEN WITCHERY is a magical practice virtually everyone can participate in. Really, if you have access to a kitchen, ingredients and a few basic tools, you're more than halfway to becoming a kitchen Witch. Kitchen Witchery is deceptively easy at first, and yet may become a serious and profound practice that brings magic from the realm of imagination and occasional high rituals into your home and daily workings through food.

Here are three simple activities that will make every meal, every gathering in your kitchen, a magical act.

Stirring your coffee or tea: almost everyone starts the day with a morning drink. Most often, it's coffee or tea,

but regardless of which drink you choose, you can make the first sip of the new day magical. When you've poured your drink into a cup or glass, begin stirring it clockwise. As you do, concentrate on the day ahead. What's on your to do list? Where are you headed off to? Who will you meet today? Keep stirring. Focus on the best outcomes for the day. Imagine each interaction throughout your day going as smoothly as possible, bringing you the most joy, generating income for you, or whatever it is that best represents a good day. Stirring clockwise brings the magic towards you. You are asking your guides, your allies, the gods and the magic in the world to support you today. You've transformed your morning coffee into a magical elixir!

Making your kitchen sacred: treat your kitchen like it is a temple to food, cooking, good health and good times. When you clean your kitchen, imagine you're sweeping the temple. Handle your ingredients with care and reverence, no matter what they are. Someone grew them, watered them, raised them, fed them, picked them, packaged them, loaded them onto a truck or stocked them on the shelf. Consecrate your kitchen tools like you would magical tools. Kitchen knives become athames. Wooden spoons become wands. Pots and pans and bowls become cauldrons. Magical tools make magical meals!

Honoring your ancestors: everyone has ancestors. There's a line of people standing behind you, stretching back through time. There are ancestors of the Craft too, those people who founded Witchcraft traditions and passed along the magic to the next generation. You can create meals in their honor all year long. Cook the food your ancestors would have eaten, or pull out the old recipe book with your grandmother's secret meatloaf recipe hidden inside. Set the table with family treasures, photos, and magical items that connect you in some meaningful way to the people you hold dear.

Kitchen magic happens every time you step into your temple and decide to make magic. So go make some magic today!

—GWION RAVEN

Pre-History of Magical Development, a Series of Unfortunate Events

"And the light shineth in darkness; and the darkness comprehended it not"

—John 1:5

TO TRULY UNDERSTAND the emergence of the concepts that arise in today's western magic, cast your attention far back in time to the cradles out of which those concepts emerged: North Africa, Western Asia, the Near East and Caucasus region, and Europe. To understand why they emerged as they did, where they did and what their focus was, we have to look at the conditions from which those cradles themselves emerged. Religion and magic evolve from cause and effect, from the human response to the world.

If instead you only look back a thousand years for the roots of magic, you miss the point of the exercise. Finding such roots means to look far beyond the organized religions and magical practices of bygone cultures— look at what made these distant ancestors tick, the cauldron of human thought and response to circumstance that birthed magic in the first place.

If you look at human nature in its most bare form, you will find two dynamics at play: find food and store food. These

114

are base survival mechanisms that along with breeding and predatory behavior keep the species alive. Those base mechanisms are still within humankind today as individuals and as societies— much of what people do has roots in those basic survival instincts. Marketing in modern consumer society taps into the finding and storing mechanism— people buy, consume and acquire more than they need.

When it comes to the deeper spiritual side of humanity, people reach out to the unknown to try and make sense of the universe. This is reaching out for spiritual food to eat for the soul. Religion and beliefs arise from trying to store spiritual food for the future. Magic is the active step that grew out of very early religious behavior in its most primal form, moving from passive acceptance of existence to actively engaging with the universe, and to maintaining an element of control in navigating through life not only for survival but in order to flourish.

Magic and its forms

Today the same as a thousand years ago, magic falls into roughly two categories: securing resources—finding food—and clearing the path ahead for the future— storing food. Magic has developed into specific acts designed to attract, repel, bind and release—base actions to gain our needs and wants. This is called results magic or low magic, but these labels are both confusing and not entirely correct.

These two labels are modern tags using modern language that both denigrate that type of magic and also limit the understanding of it. The term "results magic" comes from a 20th century model of science in which experiments are designed and implemented to not only achieve results, but to have them repeated in a stable manner. That is fine for science but magic often does not work in such clearly defined parameters. It is as unpredictable as the weather. This term likely slid into use as an attempt to give magic modern credibility by using terminology more commonly used in science.

The same can be said of the term "low magic"—the term is loaded with snobbery and high handedness. "High magic" is a term used to describe magic that reaches into mystical exploration, whereas low magic seeks to acquire something or stop something. Indeed, low magic can cause gaping potholes and potential meltdowns when it is paired up with emotional immaturity, a modern consumer mentality, magical ignorance or incompetence and a massive or fragile ego. However, magic is magic, and every type of magic has its place and function. The key is to understand what is appropriate and when. This type of magic is about survival, about finding food for the body and soul to keep them functioning, whatever a person decides that food is or represents.

High magic or mystical magic seeks the divine in the universe. It moves beyond finding and storing food, but in order to understand, and work within that type of magic, low magic must also be understood not only intellectually but practically. It is the weaving of inner power to manifest a controlled change in fate patterns. The magic itself, high or low, is no different be it mystical or functional. It is only the approach and intention that creates a line of distinction.

Continuity

This is a very important point to think about when looking into the ancient history of magic, as life in 7000 B.C.E. was very different from life today. The quest for mystical magic is a luxury in many ways—to embark upon such a journey of transformation and connection to the divine, you need food in your stomach, a roof over your head and shoes on your feet. You need to be relatively safe and secure, and have time to ponder, to think and to act. It is those luxuries out of which high magic and all mystical and philosophical thought grew.

Functional magic grew out of dire need and is essentially folk magic. It is the magic of the ordinary person trying to get by in a way that they define for themselves. Hence it is more common in poor and rural communities both today and in the past. Simply understanding the dynamics of resources and human need can put a lot of magical history into perspective.

This is not to say that mystical magic did not exist in very ancient times. There are few books left from thousands of years ago, but what does exist is magical knowledge today. Practical working magicians can look deep into the ancient past in history and recognize certain acts that left archaeological findings for us to discover. We may not know the details but the core magical mechanisms that are evident in very ancient findings show both mystical and functional magical religious behavior. It is through those behaviors that you can begin to understand yourself as a magician today and understand where your magic comes from.

When you look at ancient historical events that were happening at the same time as the emergence of magical behaviors, you can then start to understand not only the cause and effect of the development of magic, but can also the foundational understanding of magical practice today. That knowledge is a whisper that travels down through time and reminds us of our magical roots.

—JOSEPHINE MCCARTHY

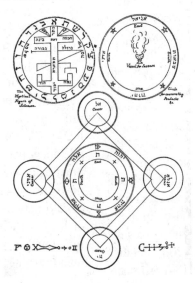

LUPTON

A Curious Pilgrim Book of Remedies

THE HISTORICAL FACTS of the Pilgrim Story, from its beginnings in Scrooby to the successful planting of Plymouth Colony, are familiar to us all. Certainly there are many small points and details that are unclear or debatable, but we probably know as much about what the Pilgrims *did* as we do about the actions of any community in the past. Because they are our ancestors and their story is so familiar, we may assume that we have a clear and accurate understanding of them personally. I can assure you that we do not. We know their history, but we do not necessarily know *them*, their opinions, their tastes and their beliefs. We are separated from the Pilgrims by the great cultural shifts that have occurred since their time— the Age of Reason, the Scientific Revolution and perhaps even this latest "post-modern" shift in public sentiment. As has often been quoted (from L. P. Hartley), "the past is a foreign country, they do things differently there." The Pilgrims were not simply ourselves wearing funny clothes and lacking the comforts of modern industrialized society. They did not share our scientific view of the world and our commonsense opinions of what constitutes reality. They were citizens of a culture as different from our own as any in the world today, despite the obvious fact that their culture contained the origins of our own.

One area in which this difference can be demonstrated most clearly is in the practice of medicine and healing. The Pilgrims and their contemporaries were heirs of several thousand years of traditional medical practices and beliefs, traditions that have little or nothing in common with our modern scientific approach to disease and treatment. For example, they had no reservations about the belief that the stars in the heavens could have a direct effect on the health of the individual and that earthly medicines had astrological virtues. The concepts which informed their understanding of the human body and the material cosmos were intricately connected. The four Elements of the external world were mirrored by the four "humors" of human physiology, not metaphorically but in fact. Herbal medicines—and for that matter, foods—were classified not for their chemical constituents or calories and carbohydrates but by their "humoral" characteristics. They were

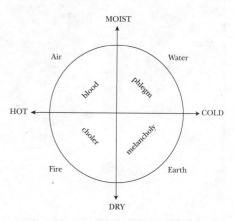

either hot or cold and either moist or dry. These qualities were not literal temperatures or moisture contents but rather the hypothetical equivalents of the four humors which constituted the human body: sanguine (hot and moist), choler (hot and dry), phlegm (cold and moist) and melancholy (cold and dry). A person's health depended on the proper balance of these four qualities, and disease was largely attributed to their imbalance. If an individual had too much choler, her symptoms would be a fiery complexion, fever, anxiety, anger and excess nervous energy. Too much melancholy and she would have a dull or sallow complexion, bags under the eyes, depression (even to the point of insanity), suffer through wasting away and lassitude or sullen and brooding resentment.

Clinical medicine was dedicated to restoring health by correcting the natural balance (or complexion) of the humors. This could be done in part physically by eliminating a certain quantity of blood so that the excess humor would then be drained away as well, or by purging the digestive system with emetics and laxatives to the same effect. On the other hand, the inadequate humor could be built up by eating the right foods and taking appropriate medicines. However, popular medicine was not limited to the classic herbal or organic medicines and bleeding, but included a large number of traditional remedies which had not any apparent humoral rationale. These were passed down orally, in medical texts and even cookbooks, but especially in those

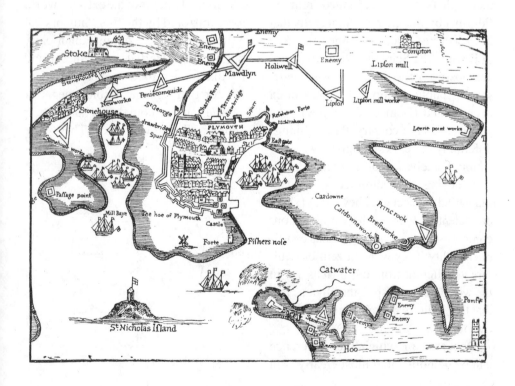

manuscript or printed collections known as "books of secrets."

It is interesting to note that the Pilgrims owned and treasured one of these handbooks of traditional medicine, Thomas Lupton's *A Thousand Notable Things,* published in 1586. It enjoyed a number of editions, there being one as late as 1815. Nevertheless, Lupton's "receipts" appear quite strange to modern sensibilities and unmistakably illustrate the chasm that separates our worldview from that of our ancestors. Lupton is one of the few medical texts the Pilgrims had that was identified by title. The book first turns up in Samuel Fuller's probate inventory in 1633, and then in William Brewster's in 1644, indicating that the book was absorbed into Brewster's library after Fuller's death. Its successive possession by the Deacon and the Elder of the Pilgrims would attest to the book's acceptability in the eyes of the community even if they might choose to ignore certain of the more questionable remedies.

Paraphrasing professor Matthew Dickie's description in *Magic and Magicians in the Graeco-Roman World*, the formulas described by Lupton are *to our eyes* quintessentially magical. This is so for two reasons: the procedures and ingredients look to us to be unscientific and thus magical, since we cannot imagine how they could be credible or effective; and we are presupposed to assume that anything astrological or "occult" must of its nature be magical and religiously illicit. This latter assumption makes no allowance for the possibility that to the Pilgrims these ideas did not have the same connotations as they do for us. Our intuitions and "commonsense" opinions of what constitutes magic and occultism are not necessarily the same as those of the educated 17th century Englishman. As Dickie points out, the centrally defining characteristics of magic are secrecy and its illicit nature. While Lupton and other authors of books of secrets and formulas are ostensibly revealing hidden or "occult" knowledge, it is clear that they do not think there is much that is dangerous about either the recipes or their publication. The fact that the Pilgrims' religious leaders valued such a book indicated that they were correct.

A Thousand Notable Things is divided into ten books with a hundred remedies and anecdotes in each. We will select a dozen from each book that best illustrate the medical beliefs of the time. The numbers at the head of each entry indicate the book, the remedy and the page it is found on. It is not the individual examples that are important, however, but the overall intellectual context that established and legitimized these strange medical recipes. They offer us a glimpse into the minds and beliefs of our ancestors in a way that simply reading the letters and chronicles of the history of Plymouth Colony cannot, and allow us to appreciate the ways in which our culture differs from as well as resembles that of the first colonists.

—SUMMANUS

TROLLDOM

TROLLDOM IS A living folk magic practice which can be documented back to the 1600s and traced back as far as the 900s. A living tradition is a practice that is currently in use and has been passed down over many generations, expanded upon and refined. There are only a limited number of living magical traditions accessible to English speaking audiences. In America, the most common three are the southern folk magic practices of Hoodoo and Appalachian Granny Magic, and the Pennsylvania Dutch tradition of Powwow.

Origins and revival

More than three million Swedes, Danes, Finns and Norwegians moved to America between the 1600s and the first two decades of the 1900s. They brought their charms and traditions to the colony of New Sweden, between 1638 and 1655 along the Delaware River in what is now Delaware, New Jersey and Pennsylvania. In the mid 1800's even more colonies of Scandinavian immigrants would settle in Pennsylvania, Minnesota, Michigan, Wisconsin, Nebraska and Illinois.

Johannes Björn Gårdbäck spent more than a decade gathering hundreds of spells for the 2015 text *Trolldom: Spells and Methods of the Norse Folk Magic Tradition.* Translated from Swedish, Norwegian, Finnish and Danish, it brings another stream of living tradition to the English speaking magical community. The practice of Trolldom includes traditional methodologies used across many cultures, as well as practices unique to Scandinavia.

Makt and tydor

A practitioner of Trolldom perceives and manipulates *makt*, or power, and *tydor*, signs. The meaning that a practitioner comes to understand about a situation has power. This makt, which manifests through tydor, has the ability to affect, influence and shape perceived reality. Through these two mechanisms the Trolldom practitioner comes to diagnose a situation and understand the forces at work. They are then able to craft and power their charms and formulas specific to a client's needs.

Tydor expands upon the familiar practice of performing divination before

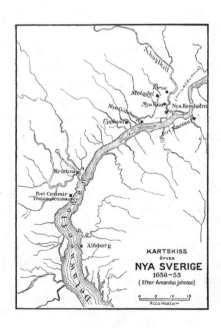

KARTSKISS
ÖFVER
NYA SVERIGE
1638−55
(Efter Amandus Johnson)

beginning spell work. Divination can help a practitioner understand the scope of the situation and the forces at work within. For example, if a partner isn't being intimate and won't talk to you about it, the problem could be caused by another lover, stress at work, or perhaps a physical issue. Diagnosing a situation is a vital part of determining what work should be done. Knowing why the partner is not being intimate allows you to choose the condition to treat: love spell for a wandering spouse, peace at home to reduce stress, control work to quiet down a pushy boss, unjinxing a tied up nature or maybe off to the doctor for some blood work.

Troll formulas

Troll formulas are spoken spells. *Galdr*, rune magic, and *runa*, runes or spell casting, come from the same origins as chanting spell formulas. The term *galdralag* refers to a style of poetic verse associated in the Eddas with magic. The identification of galdr as rune magic comes from the Galdrabok, an Icelandic grimoire dating to the 1600s. The inclusion of Christianized formulas grants us a fascinating glimpse into how older charms were transmuted into a post-pagan world.

Trolldom is one of a very few historical magical practices that not only encourages new practitioners to write their own spells, but practically requires it. In this tradition, once a mentor teaches a student a formula it no longer works for the teacher. Consequently there are hundreds of written formulas as well as various methods for constructing new formulas.

−LAURA RIVERA

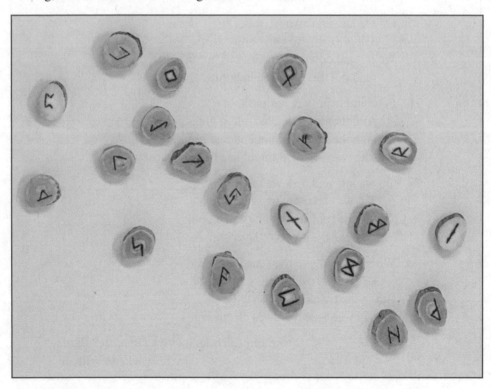

1. As I was wa'king all alone,
     Between a water and a wa,
   And there I spy'd a wee wee man,
     And he was at least that ere I saw.

2. His legs were scarce a shathmont's length,
     And thick and thimber was his thigh;
   Between his brows there was a span,
     And between his shoulders there was three.

3. He took up a meikle stane,
     and he flag't as far as I could see;
   Though I had been a Wallace wight,
     I couldna liften't to my knee.

4. "O wee wee man, but thou be strang!
     O tell me where thy dwelling be?"
   "My dwelling's down at yon bonny bower;
     O will you go with me and see?"

5. On we lap, and awa we rade,
     Till we came to yon bonny green;
   We lighted down for to bait our horse,
     And out there came a lady fine.

6. Four and twenty at her back,
     And they were a' clad out in green;
   Though the King of Scotland had been there,
     The warst o them might hae been his queen.

7. On we lap, and awa we rade,
     Till we came toy on bonny ha,
   Whare the roof was o the beaten gould,
     And the floor was o the cristal a'.

8. When we came to the stair-foot,
     Ladies were dancing, jimp and sma,
   But in the twinkling of an eye,
     My wee wee man was clean awa.

From *English and Scottish Popular Ballads*
by R. Adelaide Witham

Merry Meetings

A candle in the window, a fire on the hearth,
a discourse over tea...

ALTHOUGH I had corresponded with Raymond Buckland for almost a year before, the first time I met him was at a comedy night he was hosting in a hotel bar in rural Ohio. His best friend at the time, Bill, was the director for his local library and Ray took it upon himself to create a charity event to raise money for the local book mobile. "This is your problem now," I remember him saying as he handed me his infamous "demon in the box," and that was just the first real indication of just how funny this man really was.

I'd been aware of the legendary Raymond Buckland since the mid 1990s, but I wasn't prepared for how kind and generous he would be. One of the things he was very generous with was his archives, and in those archives are interviews from the middle of what we love to call the six-six-sixties, the real birth of the occulture that still really exists today.

Ray's gone now, but his words still exist. The kind people at *The Witches' Almanac* asked me to compile the best of some of the interviews that we have transcribed from decaying reel to reels. In these interviews you'll find a man very driven and confident, quick to correct misconceptions of the religion he had found giving him not just joy but meaning.

The interviews are not credited, but read the first batch and you'll notice the interviewer and the questioners use a very confrontational tone. You will find Ray holds his own with dignity and respect for all involved. The questioners are in italics. The second batch is a much more respectful affair, but please read these not as you would now, but as a time capsule of when anything outside of the Abrahamic structure would be considered extremely exotic.

STEVEN INTERMILL

DIRECTOR OF THE BUCKLAND MUSEUM OF WITCHCRAFT & MAGICK, CLEVELAND, OH

There's a possibility your blood may curdle, but if they if they are what they claim to be, you then have a full explanation for a reason to not accept your telephone calls. It's because they may have done something to the lines... I'd like to present to you Mr. Raymond Buckland, the High Priest of the New York Coven of Witchcraft. This Warlock operates the Buckland Museum of Witchcraft & Magick in Brentwood, NY, and that may soon disappear.

Mr. Raymond Buckland, or may I call you Ray, or Raymond, or Warlock or Oo-ee-oo whatever?

Ray or Robat would be appropriate.

Robat? What's a Robat?

Robat is my Witch name.

Like I said, which name?

My Craft name.

Your Craft name. You're British?

Yes.

How about that? Does the last syllable have anything to do with Witchcraft?

Nothing especially, no.

Because bats are often associated with eerie things, and you two are among the eeriest people I've ever seen, really.

You could spell it backwards and get Tabor, which is one of the musical instruments, traditional musical instruments used by Witches as dancing.

That's one of the most fascinating facts I've ever received...There's a gentleman at the podium that certainly must have something to say.

Gentleman, what is your name?

Bill. Sir, Mr. Buckland, have you ever heard of Sibyl Leek from England?

I have indeed, yes.

I understand there is some kind of rift going on between your coven and hers, because your covens do not recognize each other.

I would but Sybil Leek isn't here. Miss Leek was here some months back and I did speak with her then, and I feel we...

I recall the incident, and they cast spells against each other. By the way sir, are you a Warlock?

I am a member of a coven, and...

Is that American or National league?

American.

✖

The next interview is from much more of a seeker type, the questions much less condescending and much more exploratory.

✖

It's 16 minutes after 9:00 on WGLI, and we are talking to Raymond Buckland and we are talking about Witchcraft. We have a caller on the line with a question.

Yes, I have a question for Mr. Buckland, I feel like someone has put a spell on me, and how do you know for sure?

I guess my question would be is why do you think someone has put a spell on you?

Why? Well things that have been happening to me, weird things, and I knew someone that was involved in Witchcraft and that's why I think it's true.

Well first of all, Witches don't go around casting spells on people.

They don't, okay…

This would be magick. Magick in itself is a practice anyone can do it—Witch, Christian, Jew or atheist or whoever—it's not part of Witchcraft per se. Without knowing specifics, not sure if I can advise you, so many ways to work magick and so many ways to counteract it.

Is there a pin or pendant I can wear to counter act it?

Well, you could wear what is called a talisman, which is essentially a lucky charm to counter act this.

Where can I get one?

At a risk of sounding commercial you could get one at my museum which is in Bay Shore. There's a wide selection of talismans there, talisman for protection, some for love, for success in business—there are all sorts.

Our guest is Raymond Buckland, and our topic of conversation is Witchcraft. We've spoken about a lot of things but we haven't had a chance to talk about the difference between a white Witch and black Witch, and those that fall in between, the grey Witches.

Well first of all they aren't all Witches. A black Witch is actually a contradiction, the confusion is in magic—you can have black white, grey magicians. Magick is a practice in itself—anyone can do it, anyone can attempt to do it, let's put it that way. If you do it for good there's white magick, bad black magick. Of course this has nothing to do with race, these are labels from thousands of years ago, these are labels fixed thousands of years ago.

So if a person wants to work evil, a black magician, in Witchcraft there is a belief in a threefold return, a threefold retribution in this life—rather than wait until you die to get your rewards or punishment, you receive them in this life. If a person wants to work evil she will also get back three times as much evil. Due to this belief a Witch wouldn't do evil. So there is no such thing as a black Witch, but there are black magicians. There are any number of shades of grey, many fields of magick, many magical rites that could be done that could not be labeled strictly good or bad, they would fall into the fields of grey.

There was a man who lived by himself who had a fine garden of which he was very proud, a number of fruit trees, and he had a new neighbor move in next door to him. The whole family moved in. They had moved out from Brooklyn. There were three or four teenage boys that ran riot throughout the neighborhood, they played havoc with this poor man's gardens, ruined his apple trees. At one point he had to go out on family business, and was in terror of what would happen to his garden until he came back. He happened to know somebody who knew somebody that knew some Witches, and through these people he asked the Witches to do some-

praying to God, he found let's try the other side and prayed to the devil instead. So this he did, finding he never got anything from this either, but at least he felt he was fighting the establishment. Satanism came into being as an anti-Christian thing, very much a parody, instead of the Catholic mass, a black mass, instead of good, do evil. This is separate from Witchcraft, which is simply a non-Christian religion. Witches don't even believe in the devil.

Now does Witchcraft exist in places the devil doesn't exist, like China let's say.

I believe it does, and probably doesn't carry the label Witchcraft. Let's look from the derivation of the word Witch. Witch comes from an Anglo Saxon term, Wicca, which means the wise ones. This [is] simply because the leaders of the Old Religion would have to actually be wise. They were not only the priests, but would have been the doctor, veteran, lawyer. In such areas as China, you get beliefs, you get religions that are similar to the Craft as I know [it], but probably bears a different label. In Witchcraft we worship a God as well as Goddess. In China you have Guanyin which is similar to the Goddess we worship. So there are similarities, yes.

I would like to ask about Covens.

Coven, yes, well, let's look at the format of Witchcraft, since Witchcraft is a religion and is a question of a people that get together for worship. It has leaders, a high priest and high priestess that get together. This represents the deities of Witchcraft, the God and Goddess. Let's briefly review the deities of Witchcraft. It is a polytheistic religion, a belief in many

thing to guard his garden while he was away. When he had returned two weeks later, for some unknown reason the family had decided to move back to Brooklyn. So they moved back and left his garden intact. This was magick that was done to make the move to protect the old man's garden? You could not really say it was White or Black magick, but slightly white in so far as it helped the old man. Without knowing how the move would really affect the family you couldn't say it was black or not, so I would put it in the shades of grey.

Are Witches in league with the devil?

There is no such thing as Witches in league with the devil. There is something called Satanism. Satanism is quite separate from Witchcraft. Satanism is something that sprang up in the early Middle Ages as a revolt against the harshness of the church at that time. The church was very much down on the common man, the serf, the farmer, and they had nothing to call his own. Finding he was getting nothing by

Gods. And going way back to early man, the most important deities were the God of hunting and the Goddess of fertility. In those days in paleolithic times 25,000 years ago, hunting was most important to man's existence. Fertility was of course also as important—more animals that live would bring more success to the hunt. So the God of hunting and the Goddess of fertility were the main ones, and come through today. No obviously we aren't as concerned with success in the hunt today, so the God of the hunt became a God of nature generally. The Goddess of fertility [is] looked upon now as a Goddess of birth and rebirth. These are the two deities represented by a priest and priestess—they lead a coven.

A coven can consist of any number of people, it does not have to be 13 like you sometimes read. A coven can be any number, if you have a high priestess to lead them. You can have two people, you could have 200 people. What really governs the size is the physical size of your meeting place, Witches meet within a circle which is traditionally nine feet in diameter, with an altar in the center. You can find you can squeeze a dozen people in comfortably with elbow room. So a dozen with a high priestess gives you the traditional 13.

One of the things associated with Witchcraft is the nudity aspect and the orgy aspect and the power that is raised.

Right, well first of all the nudity aspect and the power. Witches believe everyone has power within them, the power comes from the power itself, it can be drawn off. Not all Witches, but most Witches work primarily naked, what they call skyclad,

clad in the sky. They work naked so they can draw this power from any area of their body, not so they can have wild orgies or anything like that. They can draw off this power easily naked. If they are fully clothed they would have to draw off the hands or the face. They would have to work a lot harder and longer to get the same amount of power.

Now the idea of sex orgies, now sex has no part of the rituals as we know them today, but again going back four, five hundred years, sex was involved, because again man was very involved in fertility, the fertility of the crops especially. Unless he got good crops he would have a hard time. So you would have rituals where a farmer and wife would have intercourse in the first farrow of a field, the first they ploughed, insuring the field would be fertile. You got a good deal of this sort of thing going on in a religious sense. These days we don't have to have sex to make sure there's food in the supermarket. Unfortunately you get today pseudo covens or pseudo Witches. You get the sort that advertise in the Village Voice, come join our coven for $500 or something, you get groups forming together and calling themselves covens but use it as an excuse for wild orgies or drugs, or something like that, but these aren't true Witches.

I know they're going to hate [it], but let's get to the phones.

I have a question about the tarot cards. Is there any reason why one shouldn't use those that have writing on them to make them easier to decipher?

There's no reason, but personally I would

advise against it if you really want to get into tarot card reading. The reason being is if you start relying on the writing that is there you will find it difficult to break away. For anyone that wants to read the tarot cards I advise they pick up any of the worthwhile books on the subject, such as Paul Case's book on the tarot, perhaps A.E. Waite's book as well, Eden Gray which I believe is currently available in paperback which is very, very good. I suggest you read them through very, very carefully, than throw them away. Then go entirely by your own instinct. But having read the books you will get an idea of laying out the cards, you will get an idea on how to interpret it, but you will find it much more accurate to go by your own feelings than by going with what's written on the cards or written in the book.

There is no such thing as being taught how to read the tarot?

Oh, you can be taught, of course. You can even take classes at the museum in various aspects of the occult. We hold classes in astrology, tarot, graphology, various aspects of the occult. I myself teach two classes, one in Witchcraft, Voodoo and magick, and one in psychic development.

Are these historical classes, or practical applications on how to be become a Witch, how to read tarot?

They are all practical except for the Witchcraft, Voodoo and magick course, which is more of the historical angle. You don't sort of graduate from that course as a ready-made Witch, but you graduate with a good idea of what Witchcraft is, what Voodoo is, and you are able to practice a

certain amount of magic, such as candle burning magic.

Good morning, my question is this. I'm wondering if one of the successful traits of the so-called Witch is to be outspoken?

I would say no, most Witches are fairly reticent, much more inclined to let the other guy do the speaking and then to have them open their own minds and draw their own conclusions. I think it comes to the old adage: empty vessels make the most noise.

Okay! I thought that I might be a Witch!

I of course have found myself there, because hahahahah.

Is there any test or anything? So you can see if you are a Witch or not?

Yes, whether you have gone through the ceremony which makes you one. How do you know, for example, you are a Catholic? You of course go through a baptism, perhaps a later confirmation, you've gone through a ceremony that makes you a member of that religion. For certain, in Witchcraft you go through a ceremony that makes you a member of the religion.

The Geomantic Figures: Albus

GEOMANCY IS AN ANCIENT SYSTEM of divination that uses sixteen symbols, the geomantic figures. Easy to learn and use, it was one of the most popular divination methods in the Middle Ages and Renaissance. It remained in use among rural cunning folk for many centuries thereafter, and is now undergoing a renaissance of its own as diviners discover its possibilities.

The geomantic figures are made up of single and double dots. Each figure has a name and a divinatory meaning, and the figures are also assigned to the four Elements, the twelve signs of the Zodiac, the seven Planets and the nodes of the Moon. The dots that make up the figures signify their inner meanings: the four lines of dots represent Fire, Air, Water and Earth and show that the elements are present in either active (one dot) or latent (two dots) form.

The third of the geomantic figures is Albus, which means White. Yes, it's Dumbledore's first name, and if you remember that you already know a good deal about it. (Hagrid's first name, Rubeus, is also a geomantic figure, and it's just as fitting.) Albus belongs to the element of Air, the Zodiacal sign Gemini, and the planet Mercury. The arrangement of dots in Albus symbolizes an empty cup standing on its base, as though waiting to be filled.

Read as symbols of the Elements, the dots that form Albus reveal much about the nature of this figure. The first, second and fourth lines, counting from the top, all have double dots, indicating that the energies of fire, air and earth are latent. The third line has a single dot; even though this is a figure of Air, the receptive element of Water is its only active element.

In divination Albus stands for peace, wisdom and purity. It is relatively weak, however, and where it appears you may need help from other people. It favors quiet progress and the use of intelligence, and so is favorable in most business questions. It is also favorable for beginnings. It is unfavorable whenever courage and decisive action are needed, or in any situation involving turbulence and rapid change.

—JOHN MICHAEL GREER

The Divining-Rod

It is a matter of common knowledge that certain expert "finders," as they are called, use a divining-rod for detecting underground springs in New England; in Pennsylvania for the locating of oil springs; and in the mineral regions of the Rockies for the discovery of hidden veins of valuable ores. The Cornish miners, also, have long made use of the divining-rod, or "dowsing-rod," as they call it, for like a purpose. A further research, probably, might reveal a similar practice in other countries; but for our purpose it is enough to present two of the most intelligent in the world as giving it their sanction and support. Various implements are employed by the expert operator in his quest for what lies hidden from mortal eyes; but the preferred agent is usually a bough of Witch-Hazel, branching at one end like the tines of a pitchfork. Taking firm hold of each prong, with the palms of the hands turned upward, the operator slowly walked around the locality where it is desired to find water; and when he reaches the right spot, presto! the free end of the bough is bent downward toward the ground as if by some invisible force, sometimes so strongly that the operator is unable to overcome it by putting forth his whole strength. "Dig here," he says, with positive assurance that the water will be found not far below the surface of the ground.

On the face of it, this performance comes rather near to our idea of a miracle than anythinger we can now call to mind. Certainly, Moses did no more when he smote the rock of Scripture. Very possibly, former generations of men may have associated the act with the operation of sorcery or magic. An enlightened age, however, accepts neither of these theories. We do not believe in miracles other than those recorded in Scripture; and we have renounced magic and sorcery as too antiquated for intelligent people to consider. Yet things are done every day which would have passed for miracles with our forefathers, without our knowing more than the bare fact that, by means of certain crude agents, obtained from the earth itself, messages are sent from New York to London under the Atlantic Ocean in a few minutes; that the most remote parts of the habitable globe have been brought into practically instantaneous communication, the one with the other; and that public and private conveyances are moving about our thoroughfares without the use of horses or steam. All these things looked to us like miracles, at first, yet custom has brought us to regard them with no more wonder than did the lighting of the first gas lamp the pedestrian of forty odd years ago. Much as we know, there is probably yet much more that we do not know.

The methods employed in finding oil springs or "leads" of ore are very similar to those made use of in discovering water. It is a fact that some of the most productive wells in the oil regions were located in this manner.

It is a further fact, that from time to time, search for buried treasure has been carried on in precisely the same way. Now some astute critics have said that the divining-rod was a humbug, because when they have tried it the mystic bow would not bend for them. It is, however, doubtful if any humbug could have stood the test of so many years without exposure, or what so many witnesses stand ready to affirm the truth of be cavalierly thrust aside as a palpable imposture.

Although I have never seen the operator at work, myself, I have often talked with those who have, whose testimony was both direct and explicit. Moreover, I do know of persons who continue to ply this trade (for no more than this is claimed for it) in some parts of New England today. Whether it should be classed among superstitions may be an open question after all.

–SAMUEL ADAMS DRAKE
The Myths and Fables of Today

A Magician's Only Essential Tool:
Their Own Human Body

(Notes Toward a General Theory of Magic, Part 5)

IT IS A TRUISM among actors that with sufficient skill they can make any play come alive for the audience on a bare stage, without scenery, props or even costuming beyond the plainest of leotards (merely for modesty's sake). Their bodies alone suffice them.

Of course, these actors' bodies are not silent and motionless on stage as they perform that play. They move, they speak, they use postures and poses and facial expressions to communicate—and to commune!—with their audience. And, with sufficient skill, they can cause the audience to perceive the characters of the play as complete human beings. While the play is going on, these characters become living people who are every bit as authentic to the audience in the theatre as their own theatre-going companions will be, back on the street after the play has let out.

As with theatre, so with magic.

With sufficient skill, human magicians need no props, no tools, no robes and cords to work magic. All they need is their own human bodies. Of course, effective scenery, props and costuming make magic easier to work—though sometimes less powerful. But these things are not strictly necessary.

A well-acted play is never just a fantasy, just an escape from reality into some kind of cloud-cuckoo-land. It is a true experience, and sometimes it is even a life-changing experience. Drawing parallels between theatre and magic is by no means dismissing magic as a fantasy or an escape from reality. Like theatre, magic done with sufficient skill can change lives—and not merely the magician's own life.

Magic, attention and the body

The fourth part of this series of *Notes* hinted that paying attention is the key skill required of every successful magician. It also noted that few things can rivet a person's attention as firmly as a well-told story of great power, and especially the sort of story that tells of "things that never happened, but always are" (to quote the Neo-Platonist philosopher Sallustius). These are the kind of stories that are embodied in myths and in their accompanying rituals. Theatre finds its ancient origins precisely in such myths and rituals.

Now what, exactly, happens when attention is riveted, while a person is watching a play, or hearing a myth or participating in a ritual of such great power? Is it the mind alone that is riveted? Hardly! On such an occasion the whole body is riveted: one's senses are more tightly focused, one's breathing becomes caught up in patterns of the experience, fidgeting ceases and restlessness abates. Riveted attention is a whole-body experience. And magic, in its greatest power, is just such an experience of riveted attention: it seizes the whole body.

Moreover, it is not only the body of the magician that is so powerfully affected. Under certain circumstances, skillfully managed, it can also be the body of a human target of the magic that will be just as powerfully affected. Let us retell a story that makes this point clear. I take it from William Seabrook's 1940 *Witchcraft, Its Power in the World Today*. It may have been fictionalized to some degree, but it can still serve our purpose here.

Seabrook's story

Stripped of irrelevant details, the story begins simply.

Back in the days of rampant colonialism, when European powers openly exploited the indigenous peoples of other continents, a European trader set up his station in a remote village, and proceeded to oppress the villagers beyond what they were willing to bear. Yet it was not safe simply to drive the trader away or openly kill him: severe reprisals from the armed forces of the colonial powers would be sure to follow. So the villagers resorted to deadly magic.

First, they prepared a life-size image—a giant doll or poppet—of the trader, and set it up in a clearing off the beaten track. With the aid of the trader's housekeepers and servants, they dressed this poppet in some of the trader's old clothes. They also got some of his cut-off hair and some clippings from his nails,

133

and glued them to the proper places on the poppet. (Frazer's two laws of magic, the Law of Similarity and the Law of Contact, are being applied here. See Note 2 in this series of articles.)

Then at regular intervals much of the village went to that clearing and performed a ritual over and over, with passionate abandon calling down sickness, decay and death upon the poppet, and so upon the trader himself.

As Seabrook told the story, a fresh human corpse, lawfully obtained according to the customs of the land, served as the body of the poppet, and it slowly decayed during the weeks of the ritual. (This would have given the ritual a greatly heightened Coefficient of Weirdness. See Note 1 in this series of articles.)

Could the trader have remained unaware that magic was being worked for his destruction? In so small a village, hardly! He would have noticed the changed bearing of the villagers, hints of a new hope for their swift deliverance from his oppression.

But the village magicians also made sure that the trader himself was told about the ritual. It was villagers whom he thought he could trust, his servants and housekeeper, who told him—with much seeming sympathy for his plight—just what was being worked against him, and just how it was being worked.

They gave him this information in drips and drabs, bit by tiny bit, so that his imagination had to work overtime to pull all the pieces together into a coherent picture of what was being done to kill him. Of course, the trader didn't believe in magic, or at least he thought that he didn't. Wasn't he a European, a rational man? His imagination, however, wasn't so sure, especially at night, in the dark, lonely hours when all the village was asleep.

Almost every day the villagers made sure that something would remind him subtly of just what was being done to kill him. He had been told the chant used in the ritual, its simple wishes for his slow and nasty death, set to a peculiar and compelling tune and rhythm. So was it a mere accident that a boy passing by his house would whistle that same tune?

Or that a woman doing her washing nearby would beat the clothes in that same rhythm? Or that a random villager, expressing sympathy for the trader's plight, would suggest encouragingly that, as a European, the trader could not be harmed by native magic, could he? He could never be quite sure.

And so the trader slowly sickened and his body decayed; and finally he died.

What killed the trader?

He was killed by magic, of course. But how precisely did that poppet-magic work? There are a number of possibilities, and any of them can serve to make our point.

The trader's position in the village was precarious. He must have known how vulnerable he was, if only unconsciously. And this sort of vulnerability always stimulates a person's imagination. The ability to imagine where danger might be lurking is a survival skill common to all higher animals, not only humans.

The trader knew that the villagers wanted him dead, and were working poppet-magic to that end. But he had, at first, no clear picture of what they were doing to bring about his death, only small disjointed bits of information, fed to him slowly, from which he might construct a full picture of the danger that he faced. And these bits of new information did not fit easily into the European model he already had in his mind of how the world should work. This lack of easy fit stimulated his imagination further, bringing it to a fever pitch.

Samuel Johnson once remarked, commenting on the unexpected eloquence of a criminal's final appeal of his death sentence, "Depend on it, sir, when a man knows he is to be hanged in a fortnight, it concentrates his mind wonderfully"—or, in our terms, one's impending doom rivets one's attention most powerfully.

As noted above, when one's attention has been so powerfully riveted on anything, it is not simply an action of one's mind, but an experience of one's entire body, with all its complex and mysterious physiology. And whole-body experiences are also where certain uncommon features of human physiology come into play. Among them are the twin features known as the *placebo effect* and the *nocebo effect*. They are, in essence, a single feature of human physiology with two names: it is called the placebo effect when it heals the body, but the nocebo effect when it harms the body. In each case, it operates because a person's very mind is not, as it were, something like an alien residing within one's body. Rather, it is just one of the many, many things that human physiology brings into being while the body is alive.

Any one part of a person's physiology can powerfully affect the other parts of that same person's physiology. Find a way to truly rivet a person's attention on their body's functions, and you can either heal or harm that person by words and symbols alone. Obviously, there are limits to this: you can't set a broken bone by such means, or repair other mechanical damage; nor can you affect every part of human physiology. But human physiology does have its very fragile points, which a knowledgeable person can exploit to do real harm, as in Seabrook's story.

Of course, this is simply one possible explanation of the trader's death. Readers who take seriously such things as the unseen world of spirits and the power of deities can also explain the trader's death in other, less materialistic ways. Whatever explanation one might prefer, the trader ended up dead nonetheless, and it was magic that brought about his death.

Poppets

And so magic can make powerful use of *poppets*, that is, of human images or dolls used to act magically upon a person for weal or for woe. The use of poppets goes back thousands of years, and they have been found on all the inhabited continents. The life-sized poppet that figures in Seabrook's story, whether it was actually made of a corpse or from less gruesome materials, is just an extreme example. The size of the poppet seems not to matter. Since small ones are much easier to make, small ones are more frequently found by archeologists in their digs, or sometimes even by unsuspecting laypeople, perhaps as they fix up an old house or dig a new garden.

In 1836 some boys in Scotland, searching the mountain called Arthur's Seat for rabbit burrows, found a hidden niche containing 17 small wooden human figures, each in its own miniature wooden coffin. The Smithsonian has photographs of both the poppets and the coffins available at https://www.smithsonianmag.com/history/edinburghs-mysterious-miniature-coffins-22371426/. Eight of them are now kept in the National Museum of Scotland; the others have been lost. It is possible that they were made and used as magical poppets, though there is no way to be certain so long after their discovery.

Even if these particular figures were made and hidden for some non-magical purpose, poppets are very often found

buried together with other artifacts—for example, spells written on lead plates—that render it obvious they were made and used for magic. By now there are several hundred examples of such poppets in museums all the world over, and surely even more of them still remain in the places where bygone magicians once hid them away. Some of the ones in museums are far more than a thousand years old. Other magical poppets were made more recently—perhaps as recently even as last week! This is still a living tradition of magic. Poppets can still work, at least if the maker has sufficient skill and knowledge.

Looking forward

This ends the fifth of these *Notes Toward a General Theory of Magic*. There will be at least one more Note, in next year's *Witches' Almanac*.

—ROBERT MATHIESEN

For photographs of these poppets and their coffins, see:

https://www.smithsonianmag.com/history/edinburghs-mysterious-miniature-coffins-22371426/

anatomy of a witch

A Symbolic Exploration of the Witch's Body

NEWCOMERS to Witchcraft are generally eager to acquire magical tools and collect all the right stuff. Being able to look the part often helps with feeling the part, or at least gives validity to using such a label. While the tools, books, stones, bits, bones and other accoutrements certainly do have their place, the most powerful tool Witches have is their bodies. But not just their physical bodies— Witches have metaphysical anatomy as well. It is this symbolic system that aids you in more fully embodying your magic and walking your path effectively.

The anatomy of the Witch consists of five major parts: lungs, heart, bones, serpent and mind, also called the weaver. Together they encapsulate the symbolic essence that directs the Witch's path. The number five is in other magical symbols such as the iconic pentagram which is not only a symbol of protection and power, but also represents the elements Air, Fire, Water and Earth combined with Spirit.

Witch's lungs Breath is a guide and a means for interconnectivity, establishing personal presence, and perceiving invisible influences. You must own your breath, recognizing your sovereignty and power. There is a balance between what you take from the world and what you put into it.

Witch's heart The heart provides a rhythm for you to move to as you seek balance within yourself and with the world around you. The pulse of your blood feeds into ritual which helps you to communicate and find purpose in your work. Rites and workings create a pattern of forward motion on your path.

Witch's bones The bones give you strength and structure to build your practice. They hold the whispers of your ancestors and sing of the future as well. Tradition can reinforce the patterns that illuminate your path with the right balance of strength and fluidity.

The serpent The most primal part of yourself, the serpent guides you in the ways of intuition, creation, renewal and protection. Ingenuity, flexibility, sensuality and intuitive wisdom are all gifts of the serpent—if you can make peace with your animal self.

The weaver The Weaver or witch's mind is the creative cauldron that stirs everything together. The purposeful weaver remembers, guides and initiates the spark that directs your path. The witch's mind is also the divine gateway and conduit for Spirit.

Spend time with each part and contemplate what it means for you. Consider how you can use your physical body to tap deeper into your metaphysical presence. Within blood, breath and bone, you will find magic to guide your way.

—LAURA TEMPEST ZAKROFF

The Mystery of Mermaids in Mainstream Media

WHAT IS THE FIRST IMAGE that appears in your mind when you hear the word "mermaid"? Perhaps a red haired beauty singing of how she longs to be a part of the human world? Maybe you think of Daryl Hannah attempting to dry off her tail on the floor of a bathroom with a hair dryer. Instead, your mind might wander to the alluring sirens in Homer's Odyssey, Hans Christian Anderson's tragic fairytale, or even a simple two-tailed mermaid that graces the side of your coffee cup. While these creatures are all special in their own ways, each of them also allows your mind to conceive of different ideas of what a mermaid really is, as well as draws you in towards her. While her image has been drastically altered to make her fit into society's standards of beauty and intrigue, the modern portrayal of the mermaid has increased her popularity in recent years, introducing a figure of magic and mystery into day to day life.

Many stories and legends of mermaids persist from ancient times. The earliest European depiction of mermaids may in fact come from the sirens of Homer's Odyssey. The creatures that appear on Odysseus' voyage had the heads of women and the bodies of birds. The sirens' voices were so irresistible that sailors would jump overboard and attempt to swim to them, driven to the point of madness by the sound of their music. These men drowned or were otherwise killed attempting to reach the sirens, often colliding with the rocks upon which the sirens sat. Homer depicts the sirens as sinister and deceptive, painting them as one of the obstacles that Odysseus and his men must face on their journey. These femme fatales could not be resisted, being so desirable that men would die over them.

With the rise of the Christian era, an important shift occurred, as the bird-like woman became a fish-like woman. This more closely fit into the story of a sea voyage, illustrating why the sailors would jump overboard. Artistic interpretations also began to show the creature as a beautiful woman from the waist up with a fish tail from the waist down. It is from this shift that we arrive at the word "mermaid." The Christian era's new vision of the animal-woman hybrid is the origin of the European and American cultures' commonly accepted physical form of a mermaid, maintaining the overall tone of mystery and manipulative seduction.

In 1837, Hans Christian Anderson published his fairytale, entitled *The Little Mermaid*, in which a young, nameless mermaid falls in love with a human man and gives up her voice to a sea Witch in exchange for legs so that she might have a chance to win the man's heart. Although this story might seem familiar, it has a different ending than the one that today's culture is used to. The deal that the mermaid makes with the sea Witch is quite different. The mermaid has an unlimited amount of time to win the prince's heart, however, if she fails to do this she will turn to sea foam on the ocean waves and die. The prince ultimately falls in love with a human princess, and when the little mermaid is given one last chance to save herself by killing the prince, she cannot do it, showing that her love for him is pure, true and undying. She jumps off the prince's wedding ship and turns to sea foam. It is in this moment that readers sympathize with her because this mermaid's power to draw people towards her is enabled by pity.

This story somewhat changed the perception of how mermaids were viewed—no more were they all evil,

manipulative and seductive. Rather, some of them could be innocent, hopeful and morally good. This shift is the point at which not only the idea of good mermaids, but mermaids of all personalities came into play, painting them more like humans with distinct and varying traits.

In the 1984 movie *Splash* the mermaid Madison, portrayed by Daryl Hannah, comes to the human world for the first time. In this movie, the plot point of the mermaid being able to become a human at her own will arises. Touching water turns her into a mermaid, and when she dries herself she once again becomes human. Madison also states that she must go back to the sea in a certain amount of time, otherwise she will never be able to return. By giving the mermaid power over her own mythical abilities, this movie allows the mermaid to become a stronger character with more control over her destiny than earlier depictions.

The second characteristic of the mermaid in this movie is her naivete, showing her quite literally as a fish out of water. *Splash* shows Madison as innocently clueless—she does not know how to speak English or understand that she must wear clothes in public when she first arrives on land. A main part of Madison's growth is adapting to customs and traditions as she learns how to live like a human. As viewers go on this journey with Madison as she innocently experiences the human world for the first time, they become invested in her journey. Once again, the mermaid has proven her ability to draw people towards her. This movie along with all the previous incarnations of the mermaid paved the way for one of the most influential and iconic mermaids in the history of the big screen.

Ariel, the mermaid in Disney's 1989 animated feature *The Little Mermaid*, combines all the previous positive traits of the mermaid, but this version of her story also ends with her finding happiness in the human world. Disney's portrayal of this fairytale has become the primary version of the story. The plot follows Hans Christian Anderson's story closely, however the deal Ariel strikes with the sea Witch Ursula states that she will have three days to win the kiss of true love from the

prince. If she cannot achieve this, she will turn back into a mermaid and belong to Ursula, who is portrayed as an octopus-human hybrid. Like Anderson's mermaid, Ariel does not complete her goal and turns back into her original form. However, with the help of her friends, she eventually defeats Ursula and Ariel's father turns her back into a human so that she can marry the prince.

Like the mermaids before her Ariel is naive to the ways of the human world and has the traits of innocence and goodness, a beautiful and alluring voice and a fascination with a human man. Interestingly, the two qualities that mermaids possessed in earlier versions of the story but which Ariel lacks can be seen in Ursula. This sea Witch can become human at will and is manipulative and deceptive, using Ariel's stolen voice for evil—to bewitch the prince. The inclusion of all the past traits of mermaids between Ariel and Ursula pays homage to the earlier versions and creates two opposing and well rounded characters that audiences love to this day.

Different versions of her story have changed certain aspects of the mermaid, both giving and taking away her abilities. It is this very adaptability that makes her stand out from other mythical creatures and invokes such fascination from the public. Over time the mermaid has become a symbol for those who long for more than they have, as well as for those who are curious, optimistic and hopeful in life. Likewise she appeals to those who identify with the mysterious and the alluring, making her extremely likable and relatable. So the next time you see someone carrying a tote bag or wearing clothing with a mermaid on it, realize the impact that a magical figure has had over them. Even though she may only be a myth, her presence in any form still lures people towards her.

-NERITES

Mediumship for the People

MEDIUMSHIP is the practice of interacting with spirits, that is beings without a physical body. Some people assume that you have to be gifted to perform mediumship, but that's a bit like saying you have to be gifted to cook. Maybe you need to be gifted to become a chef at a Michelin star restaurant, but most cooks just need to learn the basics so they can feed themselves every day. The fact of the matter is that people are interacting with spirits all the time, whether they know it or not. How can non-gifted folks interact with awareness and respect?

In a materialist society, it's easy to assume that spirits– if they do exist– are far away from us and need to be summoned into our lives. But the spirit world and the world of matter are woven together like a grand, miraculous tapestry. There are even some spirits that you're already in contact with every day. The first step towards interacting with them consciously is simply being aware of them.

Types of spirits

You must listen to your own spirit. As the saying goes, people are not human beings having a spiritual experience, but spiritual beings having human experience. Each person came here for a reason, but that reason can't be put in words. If only it were as simple as saying, "it's my destiny to have children, become a doctor, and live in California!" Destiny isn't simple or fixed, though, so it can't be summed up in words. Instead, you must tune in to your own spirit so you can follow it through life's nonlinear experiences.

Work with the spirits of your ancestors. Blood relations are important, but ancestors are more than just that. They can also be adoptive family, stepfamily, childhood caregivers, close friends, spiritual teachers and anyone else who walked your path before you. They can be artists whose work has touched you, saints who are sympathetic to you and spirit guides who have chosen to walk with you. Ancestors will be the first spirits to help you, protect you and give you good advice. For more on how to work with them, see *Honoring Your Ancestors: A Guide to Ancestral Veneration.*

All places have their own spirits, whether you're hiking up a mountain or sitting on your living room couch. The moment you walk into a room, you have a physical and emotional response to the spirit of that place. It might feel good, bad or neutral, but it always feels like something. It's a good idea to be respectful to the spirits of the place around you, especially if you intend to spend time in that particular place regularly. Try saying thank you to the spirit of your house for giving you shelter every day and see what happens after a week.

Practicing spiritual hygiene

The word *miasma* (pollution) comes to us from Greek. It refers to the natural byproducts of life that get in the way of living if we don't clear them out of our space. Miasma can have physical form, like garbage, dust or clutter, or it can be purely metaphysical, like old habits, bad vibes or self-limiting beliefs. Spiritual hygiene is the practice of dealing with miasma, and it is your first line of defense against hostile spirits.

If you think your house is haunted, by all means call a professional for help. Otherwise simple DIY practices can keep you and your home happy, healthy and metaphysically safe. As you become more sensitive to the spiritual realm, miasma will start to make you uncomfortable. When spirits with your best interests at heart become more vocal, they'll remind you how important spiritual hygiene is. You can skip those reminders and go straight to the interesting spiritual advice by staying on top of things.

There are a few ways you might want to keep your home and body spiritually clean. Sweep your floors. There's a reason why Witches are depicted with brooms! Dirt has powerful magical properties. Every time you come home, a little dirt from all the places you visited comes with you. That's a lot of psychic noise for the space you want to be able to fall asleep in. Clean your dishes. Food waste can attract hungry ghosts, not to mention physical pests. Take regular spiritual baths. Add a pinch of sea salt and a splash of Florida water to a big bowl of warm water. Pour this over yourself after taking a regular shower.

Perceiving messages

When you ask a question, there is always a response. You might not always hear it. Minds are full of useless chattering. Buddhists call this noise the monkey mind. It consists of the scripts you have picked up from society that play on repeat all day every day. You might worry about what other people think of you, you might judge other people who remind you of yourself, or you might agonize over the past and fantasize about the future. Of course, the monkey mind chatters about spiritual work. "Did you buy the right candle? Will this altar look good on Instagram? Did you say the prayer correctly? What will the spirit say? Will it reaffirm the thing you want so badly to be true?"

Staying open is the most important thing. That means asking the monkey mind to quiet down. It means getting comfortable with silence. Receiving messages from spirit is a lot like being a reporter and interviewing a celebrity. You need to give the interview subjects a chance to fill their own silence. There are many ways to perceive messages from spirits. Most people have heard of clairvoyance, in which perception resembles physical sight. But there's also clairaudience, which resembles hearing, clairsentience, or feeling, clairscent, or smelling, clairgustance, tasting, and a whole host of other psychic experiences. Some will come to you naturally; others, you may experience only once or twice in this lifetime. Don't discount information that comes in a form other than what you were expecting. Respect the message as it comes, whether that's as a vision or as the scent of perfume or as something else entirely. If you struggle to perceive a message in the moment, remember that it can unfold over time. Pay attention to dreams and watch for synchronicities in the days following a spiritual encounter. These can shed new light on an experience that didn't immediately make sense.

Putting it all together

Just because someone is a spirit, that doesn't mean they're inherently better or wiser than you. Any message you receive from a spirit should be evaluated just like advice from a living person. If you know the source well, respect them and resonate with the message, then incorporate it into your life. But if you're still getting to know the source or the message seems odd, proceed with caution. And if you know the source well but don't respect them, it may be time to say, "thank you and good-bye."

When it comes to evaluating a message, your body is your most powerful divination tool. How did your body feel when the message was received? How does it feel now, when you sit with the message? Do you feel peaceful or tense? Does your heart feel open or closed? Peaceful, open-hearted feelings in the body are the hallmark of messages worth your attention. It's okay to disregard a message from a spirit if that message doesn't feel good in your body or isn't in alignment with your own spirit.

Spirits don't run your life for you. You contact them to assist your own spiritual growth, and that growth requires you to take responsibility for your decisions. Messages from wise spirits help you to broaden your perspective so you can make choices that benefit yourself, your community, and your descendants. Stay aware, act respectfully, and listen to your heart. These are the most powerful rituals you can perform.

—MALLORIE VAUDOISE

Close to You

WITCHES living near the coast are lucky enough to witness the daily cycle of rising and falling tides, but they may not know how these are connected to the Moon. She doesn't pull the waters along, as you may have learned. Her attractive power upon the oceans creates an unmoving bulge of water through which the land moves as Mother Earth rotates. This movement into and out of the water bulge creates the illusion of rising and falling tides.

Most places have two high and two low tides over the course of a day. The second high tide occurs because there are actually two bulges—one pointing towards the Moon, another on the far side of Earth pointing into space. The bulge nearest the Moon is subject to her strongest attraction, but the attraction weakens quickly. The center of Earth, further from the Moon, is much less attracted to her, and the far side of Earth, furthest from the Moon, is least attracted. The second bulge resides in this area of weakest attraction, as it lags behind the rest of Earth.

These leading and lagging bulges are identical and opposite, but are not composed of water alone. The land is also subject to the Moon and rises and falls, and we never notice because everything within our frame of reference rises and falls alongside us.

Mass is a characteristic property of matter. The more massive, the more attractive power matter possesses. The Moon's attractive power is nearly the same every day and night when she passes overhead and draws Earth's lands and waters to herself. Her waxing and waning may affect her beauty, but never her attractive powers. Regardless of phase, visible or not, you are pulled to her the most strongly when she is overhead, and that's a sacred spot.

—STELLUX

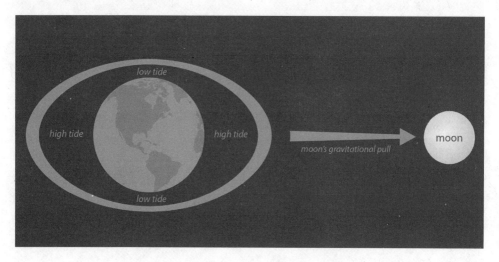

ECTOPLASM, GHOSTLY RESIDUE OR WISHFUL THINKING?

THE SEARCH for tangible proof as verified by the five senses, for the real existence of spirits, ghosts and the afterlife is a tantalizing and elusive quest. Although connections with and messages from supernatural forces have been noted since the dawn of time, the rise of Spiritualism in the mid–19th century brought a focus on seeking information and greater detail for documentation. At that time, highly sensitive individuals who served as mediators with the spirit world, known as mediums, began to materialize messages for those who longed for communication. Materializing mediumship involved manifesting visible spectral forms. These were photographed and sometimes included music or fragrances. Objects such as flowers or feathers could mysteriously float from above during gatherings called seances or sittings.

Following the Civil War, materializing mediumship became very sophisticated.

It was at that time that materializing mediums began to become conduits for a substance called ectoplasm, from the Greek words *ektos* (outside) and *plasma* (something formed or molded). The term was coined in 1894 by Charles Richet, a French physiologist, aviator, Nobel prize winner and novelist. Ectoplasm was the milky, slimy residue, smelling of ozone, which flowed from the eyes, noses, ears, mouths and other bodily orifices of mediums while they were in trance states. White veils and patches, suggestive of gauze or cheese cloth, emerged from the ectoplasm once it left a medium's body. From this background the hands, faces and limbs of spirit guides could be seen. These represented the colors, textures and memories of lost loved ones. The ectoplasm would manifest as a cloud or mass, then rise to form a pillar. One report described a tiny fairy figure with an oversized head which left the medium's

mouth, circled overhead and settled on the white mass. Sometimes the cool, gel-like ectoplasm emitted a greenish glow, while other times it remained white.

When Richet performed tests on the ectoplasm residue following seances, he compared the substance to the mucus and fat cells in the human body. In 1928 Richet summarized his studies of the subject in *Our Sixth Sense*: "When we have fathomed the history of these unknown vibrations emanating from reality—past reality, present reality, and even future reality—we shall doubtless have given them an unwonted degree of importance." This seems to hint at suspicions of fraud. Indeed, some of the vintage photographs of ectoplasm seem to include obvious cut outs from magazines or sketches, or even human accomplices draped in cloth.

Following World War II, amid numerous accusations of fraud, practitioners of Spiritualism began to de-emphasize the practice of physical mediumship. The appearance of ectoplasm became less frequent. Mental mediumship, with the medium relaying spirit messages verbally, as well as table tipping, when spiritual forces communicate through tapping or moving small tables, became popular instead. In Spiritualist circles in Germany and Australia, however, since the 1990s some new instances of materialization involving ectoplasm have been reported.

The 1984 film *Ghostbusters*, starring Bill Murray, Dan Akroyd and Harold Ramos, also revived ectoplasm again. The spectral visitors make dramatic appearances with green or white slime. Even the license plate on the Ecto-mobile, the 1959 white

Cadillac ambulance which the team of Ghostbusters drove, read "ECTO-1". The comedy classic, with its slew of ghosts accompanied by ectoplasm, has endured, so on at least some level the phenomenon seems to be very real.

Recipe For Creating Your Own Ectoplasm
Don't be surprised if it does attract para-normal energies!

2 bottles school glue, refrigerated until cold.
4 to 8 ounces liquid starch
1 teaspoon blue or green glow paint

Mix the glue and paint thoroughly. Slowly add the starch to the desired consistency and knead into a ball. Craft accents such as eyes, rubbery teeth, foam shapes, et cetera can be added. Place the ghost slime in an air-tight glass container and refrigerate it to keep it icy cold until needed.

—MARINA BRYONY

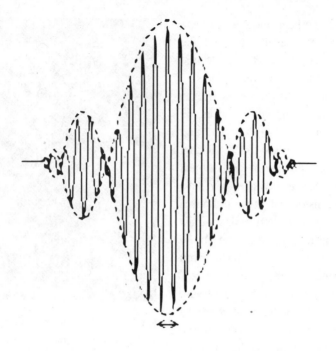

Know Matter!

THE WORK of Witchcraft is to maintain or to bring things back into balance. What exists on the physical plane is reflected on the metaphysical plane—as above so below—and the phenomenon of balance is no exception. Balance expresses itself through principles of symmetry that scientists continue to uncover. To study matter is to study balance, and to know the evolution of matter is to appreciate the workings of symmetry on both planes. In fact, the principles of symmetry suggest that the physical universe shouldn't exist at all! So why is there a material plane? What is the origin of matter?

Particles and waves

In the beginning, or shortly after the big bang, the young universe was composed of early matter. These particles are rarely found outside of physics laboratories today, and then only after an enormous amount of resources and effort have been expended to create and maintain an environment in which to study them. These early particles are collectively known as exotic matter, in contrast to the ordinary matter one sees and experiences. After the universe had aged a bit, about 300,000 years, this early or exotic matter transformed into the more familiar ordinary matter. Upon that transformation, the first energy came into existence, which expressed itself as the first light.

Both ordinary matter and light were created from the same exotic matter source, but to define the exact nature of either has proven to be elusive, a debatable point for centuries. The 17th century physicist Isaac Newton proposed that the source was, ironically, a stream of matter. His contemporary Christiaan Huygens asserted that it was a wave of energy. Current physicists consider it to be both—sometimes it exists as energy in an electromagnetic wave, other times as matter, in particles known as photons. These electromagnetic waves or photons range from the very short to the very long, and they carry various amounts of energy. That energy exerts a force on anything they should happen to encounter.

The electromagnetic spectrum

Collectively, the wide range of these waves or photons is known as the electromagnetic spectrum. One small section of the spectrum includes the colors humans perceive as visible light. Other creatures, such as bees and butterflies, can see a bit above our range into the ultraviolet, which helps them to spot flowers easily. Certain cold blooded animals, like snakes and blood sucking insects, can see a bit below our range into the infrared, and use this ability to hone in on mammalian targets.

Consider the whole of the electromagnetic spectrum to be a piano keyboard. What we see as visible light is only a couple of keys in the middle of the keyboard, but invisible light extends in a range far above and below. With certain electronic devices we can extend our sight and perceive television and radio, but we see only a very narrow range of light through our physical eyes.

Matter and energy

Like the spectrum itself, what we may perceive psychically through our third eye is much broader. Whether wave or particle, light exerts a force conveying information to us, and it is both wave and particle, energy and matter.

But energy and matter are the same thing! That is the key concept Albert Einstein put forth in his famous equation $E=mc^2$, or energy equals mass, or matter, times the square of the speed of light. Mass, by the way, is a term quantifying how much matter a body contains. Energy is on one side of the equation, matter on the other. Ponder this for a moment— energy is matter. Matter is Energy. They are one and the same, two expressions of one fundamental phenomenon, and each may convert into the other.

Although they are equal, that does not imply you get equal amounts of one thing when converting to another. The equation is balanced by

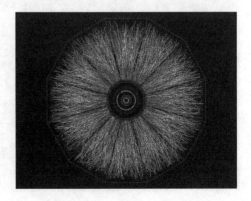

the C-squared term, which expresses how much of one value you get for an amount of the other. If you could gather a huge amount of energy, you could convert it into a tiny amount of matter. Physicists actually performed this alchemy for the first time in 1997, and like the God of Genesis, literally created a physical object from energy. Conversely, a tiny amount of matter yields a huge amount of energy. Physicists first accomplished that feat in 1942. A few years later, a single gram of matter per city, transmuted into energy, was all that was needed to vaporize 120,000 humans instantly at Hiroshima and Nagasaki and level both cities, concluding World War II.

Matter is condensed energy. Energy is dispersed matter. They are interconvertible. They are light.

Equal and opposite forces

In addition to his study of light, Isaac Newton developed laws of motion.

The familiar third law states that every force has an equal and opposite force. Specifically, it means that forces are always balanced, always exist in pairs that are equal in magnitude and opposite in direction, that is, each operating upon different things. Standing still on a sandy beach, your feet exert a force on the sand and the sand exerts a counter force on your feet in the opposite direction. The two forces balance—if they didn't, you'd either sink into the sand or levitate above it! If you started walking, the force of the sand on your feet pushes your whole body forward, while the force of your feet on the sand leaves footprints where you just stepped. If you started running, the magnitude of the two opposing forces is greater and is visibly apparent— your footprints would be farther apart and each footprint would be deeper.

These balancing and opposing forces are examples from physics, but symmetry can also appear in

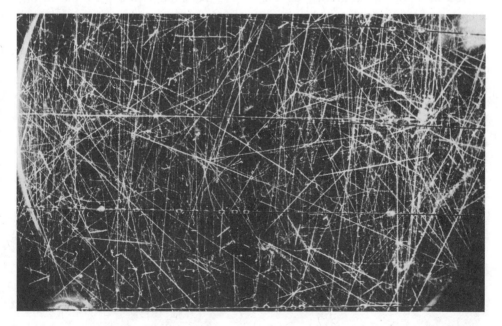

mathematics. The square root of 25 is not only 5, but also negative 5. Multiplying negative 5 by itself equals 25, as does multiplying positive 5 by itself. A positive 5 and a negative 5 are numerical values equal in magnitude but opposite in direction or in this case, opposite in value.

In physics, a force has an equal and opposite force. In metaphysics, what is put forth returns trebled. A metaphysical force is therefore an asymmetric system, as its force has not one, but three, equal counter forces. Witches, beware what you put forth!

Positive and negative charges

Symmetry is also reflected in all ordinary matter, which is composed of atoms, and every atom in existence is literally composed of electromagnetic energy, or light. This light presents in the form of subatomic particles that possess a positive, negative or neutral electric charge, named respectively proton, electron and neutron. The simplest atom, hydrogen, contains a single positive charge surrounded by a single negative charge, or a proton surrounded by an electron, each balancing the other. The next simplest atom, helium, contains two positive charges and two neutral charges, surrounded by two negative charges, or in terms of particles, two protons and two neutrons surrounded by two electrons, the two positive charges opposing and balancing the two negative charges.

Incredibly, these two elements, hydrogen and helium, compose more than 99 percent of the physical universe—the other 116 elements found on the periodic table together merely make up the remaining portion, less than one percent! The properties of each atom on the table are determined by the arrangement and number of protons and neutrons. These can be quite complex, involving dozens of protons, neutrons and corresponding electrons involved in a atom. The science of nuclear physics includes the study of such configurations. Most of the time, the number of negatively charged electrons on the outskirts of the atom exactly matches the number of positively charged protons within the nucleus. When the charges don't match, the atom attempts to restore the balance by gaining or losing additional electrons. The science of chemistry is the study of that movement of electrons between atoms.

Antimatter

Up until the 1930s all atoms were considered to be configured with negative charges surrounding positive charges. In the 1920s Paul Dirac sought to mathematically formalize the developing science of quantum mechanics. He found that his equations implied the existence of a particle exactly like an electron, but possessing an opposite or positive charge. Carl Anderson found that particle in 1932. This positive electron, or positron, was the first particle of antimatter discovered.

Since then whole classes of antiparticles have been discovered and studied. Physicists were able to create the first and simplest anti-atom, antihydrogen, in the 1990s. It consisted of a single negative charge surrounded by a single positive charge. Symmetry therefore exists between matter and antimatter atoms. In matter, negative charges surround positive charges; in antimatter, positive charges surround negative charges.

If you took an atom of anti-hydrogen and collided it with an atom of hydrogen, the electron from the hydrogen and the positron from the anti-hydrogen would both shed their physical state as particles. In accordance with Einstein's equation, they would become two highly energetic electromagnetic waves, flying off in opposite directions. The reverse may also occur—two highly energetic electromagnetic waves may collide and transmute back into an electron and positron.

The state of the universe after the first light of creation came into existence was a constant back and forth transmutation between particles and waves, where matter and antimatter became energy, and energy became antimatter and matter. This incomprehensibly immense cloud of particles, anti-particles and energy began to spread and cool. It coalesced into just about equal amounts of stable matter and antimatter. Then most of the matter and antimatter turned back into energy, but not all—if it had, we would not exist as physical beings.

For reasons scientists are still attempting to determine, one in ten billion atoms of matter survived that transformation with its antimatter counterpart. Those small surviving fragments of matter have become the entirety of the physical plane. Because our galaxy is composed of matter, there may be anti-

galaxies, although none have been detected yet. Since the existence of an all-matter universe violates the principle of symmetry, there may be an antimatter universe existing in parallel with ours.

One aspect of anti-physics in that anti-universe led Richard Feynman, who was studying wave–particle interactions in the 1940s, to conclude that a positron is an electron going backward in time. Time itself may be symmetrical! In that anti-universe, future events have already happened, and past events have yet to occur. If it exists, is there communication between the universe and an anti-universe? Could the symmetry of time be the basis for prescience?

Witches already know.

—STELLUX

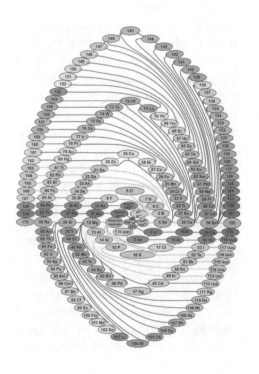

⋚ Birch ⋚

BETH

FEW TREES FIGURE more prominently in the folklore of Northern Europe than the birch. Deemed sacred to Thor, Norse god of thunder and lightning, the birch symbolizes youth and springtime. It is one of the hardiest trees in the world; growing further north, and, with the rowan and the ash, higher up mountains than any other species. The birch is called "the tree of inception" with good reason. Not only does it self-sow, forming groves, but it is one of the earliest forest trees to put out leaves in spring.

An Old English folk-ballad titled *The Wife of Usher's Well* has a line: "And their hats were o' the birch," echoing a rural theme that souls returning from the dead decked themselves with branches plucked from the birch trees surrounding the gates of Paradise. The boughs were worn for protection lest the winds of Earth discover them and thwart their mission. Medieval art often depicts a ghostly presence as a figure arrayed in birch branches.

Its uncanny nature links the tree with witchcraft. Birch is the wood of broomsticks; flying transport to the Sabbat gatherings. Oral tradition holds that witches anoint their birch rods with the words: "Away we go, not too high and not too low."

Siberian shamans may still seek the "magic mushroom" (the scarlet white-spotted fly agaric) in birch groves where it flourishes. Intoxicated by the ritually ingested mushrooms, shamans reach a state of ecstasy by climbing a birch tree and cutting nine notches in its crown.

Birch lore turns up in many cultures. The Dakota Sioux burn birch bark to discourage thunder spirits. Scandinavians carry a young dried leaf for good luck on the first day of a new job. Basque witches use birch oil to anoint love candles. A bough on the roof protects a German home from lightning strikes. Many sources claim that smoke rising from a fire of birch logs purifies the surroundings.

here is a litle folish song
known to all yett it is
a Song of a Pixy, That
is

Litel Iacke Horner
Satt in a Corner
Eating a Christmass Pye
He putt in his Thumbe
And puld out a Plumme
Loe whatt a good Boye
am I!

Now the Pixy hath hornes or
long Eares; tis all one, and the
Devill is called old Hornie
but the Pixy in a corner eating
a Pye or whatever the Housewif
giveth him is Iacke Horner
and I that yee may be sure
and bett on itt a Sixpence iff
ye have one.

154

There is a litle folish song knoun to all yett it is a Song of a Pixy, that is—

Litel Jacke Horner
Satt in a corner
Eating a Christmass Pye
He putt in his Thumbe
and puld out a Plumme
Loe whatt a good Boye am I.

Now the Pixy hath hornes or long Eares; tis all one, and the Devill is called Old Hornie but the Pixy in a corner eating a Pye or whatever the Housewife giveth him is Jacke Horner and of thatt yee may be sure and bett on itt a sixpence iff ye have one.

Moon Cycles

A New Moon rises with the Sun,
Her waxing half at midday shows,
The Full Moon climbs at sunset hour,
And waning half the midnight knows.

NEW	2022	FULL	NEW	2023	FULL
Jan. 2		Jan. 17			Jan 6
Feb. 1		Feb. 16	Jan. 21		Feb. 5
Mar. 2		Mar. 18	Feb. 20		Mar. 7
Apr. 1		Apr. 16	Mar. 21		Apr. 6
Apr. 30*		May 16	Apr. 20		May 5
May 30		June 14	May 19		June 3
June 28		July 13	June 18		July 3
July 28		Aug. 11	July 17		Aug. 1
Aug. 27		Sept. 10	Aug. 16		Aug. 30**
Sept. 25		Oct. 9	Sept. 14		Sept. 29
Oct. 25		Nov. 8	Oct. 14		Oct. 28
Nov. 23		Dec. 7	Nov. 13		Nov. 27
Dec. 23			Dec. 12		Dec. 26

*A rare second New Moon in a single month is called a "Black Moon."
**A rare second Full Moon in a single month is called a "Blue Moon."

Life takes on added dimension when you match your activities to the waxing and waning of the Moon. Observe the sequence of her phases to learn the wisdom of constant change within complete certainty.

Dates are for Eastern Standard and Daylight Time.

presage

by Dikki-Jo Mullen

ARIES, 2021–PISCES, 2022

The Sun, source of all life on planet Earth, is the theme throughout this fiftieth anniversary edition of The Witches' Almanac. The Sun sign is determined by the Earth's position in its path around the Sun on the birthday. The single most important factor in the horoscope, the Sun sign shows where and how each of us will shine and is the basis for the astrological predictions in Presage.

During these times of personal and planetary change, the influence of the Sun can also assume a sinister side, as in concerns about global warming and climate change. Combined with the Sun sign, the influences of the Moon and planets are explored in the forecasts. The idea is to build upon the powerful axiom "as above, so below" from "The Emerald Tablet," a short work well known in occult circles and attributed to Hermes Trismegistus. The celestial map above is the guide to enjoying a wholesome and successful year on Earth below.

While exploring what this means to you, start with the forecast for your Sun sign. Then read the forecast for your Moon sign, which addresses the personality, emotional needs and instinctual responses. Next turn to the forecast for your rising sign, the ascendant. That is the zodiac sign rising at the time of birth. The ascendant shows the impression you create, the way you appear to those around you.

Those born on a cusp, the day of a sign change, are advised to consult both forecasts and blend the information in ways unique to them. Here begins the fiftieth year of Presage, the astrology section of The Witches' Almanac.

Great writers and scientists such as Ralph Waldo Emerson and Isaac Newton consulted it as a way to understand how and why the universe works. Rosicrucianism, Freemasonry, Theosophy and The Golden Dawn all trace inspiration from this work.

ASTROLOGICAL KEYS

Signs of the Zodiac
Channels of Expression

ARIES: fiery, pioneering, competitive
TAURUS: earthy, stable, practical
GEMINI: dual, lively, versatile
CANCER: protective, traditional
LEO: dramatic, flamboyant, warm
VIRGO: conscientious, analytical
LIBRA: refined, fair, sociable
SCORPIO: intense, secretive, ambitious
SAGITTARIUS: friendly, expansive
CAPRICORN: cautious, materialistic
AQUARIUS: inquisitive, unpredictable
PISCES: responsive, dependent, fanciful

Elements

FIRE: Aries, Leo, Sagittarius
EARTH: Taurus, Virgo, Capricorn
AIR: Gemini, Libra, Aquarius
WATER: Cancer, Scorpio, Pisces

Qualities

CARDINAL	FIXED	MUTABLE
Aries	Taurus	Gemini
Cancer	Leo	Virgo
Libra	Scorpio	Sagittarius
Capricorn	Aquarius	Pisces

CARDINAL signs mark the beginning of each new season — active.
FIXED signs represent the season at its height — steadfast.
MUTABLE signs herald a change of season — variable.

Celestial Bodies
Generating Energy of the Cosmos

Sun: birth sign, ego, identity
Moon: emotions, memories, personality
Mercury: communication, intellect, skills
Venus: love, pleasures, the fine arts
Mars: energy, challenges, sports
Jupiter: expansion, religion, happiness
Saturn: responsibility, maturity, realities
Uranus: originality, science, progress
Neptune: dreams, illusions, inspiration
Pluto: rebirth, renewal, resources

Glossary of Aspects

Conjunction: two planets within the same sign or less than 10 degrees apart, favorable or unfavorable according to the nature of the planets.

Sextile: a pleasant, harmonious aspect occurring when two planets are two signs or 60 degrees apart.

Square: a major negative effect resulting when planets are three signs from one another or 90 degrees apart.

Trine: planets four signs or 120 degrees apart, forming a positive and favorable influence.

Quincunx: planets are 150 degrees or about 5 signs apart. The hand of fate is at work and unique challenges can develop. Sometimes a karmic situation emerges.

Opposition: a six-sign or 180° separation of planets generating positive or negative forces depending on the planets involved.

The Houses — *Twelve Areas of Life*

1st house: appearance, image, identity
2nd house: money, possessions, tools
3rd house: communications, siblings
4th house: family, domesticity, security
5th house: romance, creativity, children
6th house: daily routine, service, health
7th house: marriage, partnerships, union
8th house: passion, death, rebirth, soul
9th house: travel, philosophy, education
10th house: fame, achievement, mastery
11th house: goals, friends, high hopes
12th house: sacrifice, solitude, privacy

Eclipses

Elements of surprise, odd weather patterns, change and growth are linked to eclipses. Those with a birthday within three days of an eclipse can expect some shifts in the status quo. There will be five eclipses this year, four are partial and one is total.

May 26, 2021—Full Moon—total lunar eclipse in Sagittarius, South Node

June 10, 2021—New Moon—partial solar eclipse in Gemini, North Node

November 19, 2021—Full Moon—partial lunar eclipse in Taurus, North Node

December 4, 2021—New Moon—total solar eclipse in Sagittarius South Node

A total eclipse is more influential than a partial. The eclipses conjunct the Moon's North Node are thought to be more favorable than those conjunct the South Node.

Retrograde Planetary Motion

Retrogrades promise a change of pace, different paths and perspectives.

Mercury Retrograde

Impacts technology, travel and communication. Those who have been out of touch return. Revise, review and tread familiar paths. Affected: Gemini and Virgo

May 30–June 23, 2021
in Gemini
September 27–October 18, 2021
in Libra
January 14–February 4, 2022
in Aquarius and Capricorn

Venus Retrograde

Venus retrograde influences art, finances, and love. Affected: Taurus and Libra

December 19, 2021–January 29, 2022 in Capricorn

Mars Retrograde

The military, sports, and heavy industry are impacted. Affected: Aries and Scorpio. There will not be a Mars retrograde cycle this year.

Jupiter Retrograde

Large animals, speculation, education, and religion are impacted. Affected: Sagittarius and Pisces

June 20–October 18, 2021
in Pisces and Aquarius

Saturn Retrograde

Elderly people, the disadvantaged, employment and natural resources are linked to Saturn. Affected: Capricorn and Aquarius

May 23–October 11, 2021
in Aquarius

Uranus Retrograde

Inventions, science, electronics, revolutionaries and extreme weather relate to Uranus retrograde. Affected: Aquarius

August 20, 2021–January 18, 2022
in Taurus

Neptune Retrograde

Water, aquatic creatures, chemicals, spiritual forces and psychic phenomena are impacted by this retrograde. Affected: Pisces

June 26–December 1, 2021
in Pisces

Pluto Retrograde

Ecology, espionage, birth and death rates, nuclear power and mysteries relate to Pluto retrograde. Affected: Scorpio

April 28–October 7, 2021
in Capricorn

ARIES

March 20–April 19

Spring 2021–Spring 2022 for those
born under the sign of the Ram

Aries has a special affinity for new beginnings. An enthusiastic, enterprising adven-
turer, you are always ready to seek and
explore. However, make a habit of following through with ideas and completing the
projects you begin. Redundant situations
or negativity can bore or depress you.
Freshness and a pioneer spirit will foster
the best within you.

Venus enters your sign at the Vernal
Equinox. This is a very positive transit
lasting through April 14, favoring both
love and money. Associates are supportive. A relationship takes a turn for the
better at the Full Moon on March 28.
Mercury and Mars influences favor final-
izing plans involving travel and study during late April. Prepare a prosperity ritual
on May Day when several planets, including Uranus, highlight your financial sector. Pursue income opportunities which
are in sync with your skill set May 1–11.

Late May through mid-June your 3rd
house sets the pace. Ideas suggested by
a neighbor or sibling can offer valuable
perspectives. This points to worthwhile
invitations involving travel. The eclipse
on June 10 brings the specifics into
view. At the Summer Solstice retrograde
Jupiter accents involvement with charitable projects and righting old wrongs.

This continues as a background theme
in your life through the autumn. During
July a trine from Mars to your Sun promises added vitality and motivation. Sports,
games and creative projects brighten
the days leading up to Lammastide.
August 1–11 brings a strong Mercury influence in your 5th house. Communication
with children and loved ones is excellent.
A close partner has good news to share
from mid-August through September 10
when Venus blesses your relationship sector. A charming person exhibits unique
talents and appreciates your support in
celebrating an achievement.

As the Autumnal Equinox nears, air
sign transits shift the focus to future
plans and community involvement.
The Full Moon on September 20 highlights service. A new animal companion could enter your life near then too.
October finds retrograde Mercury rekin-
dling old relationships. Someone close
to you makes an important choice near
October 18. At the end of October Mars,
your ruler, enters your 8th house. Honor
ancestors. At All Hallows a past life rec-
ollection suggests the perfect costume
design. Throughout November psychic
connections are heightened; friendly
spirit entities hover nearby. Mid-
November promises a peak time regarding positive paranormal happenings.

December 1–13 is ideal for travel or
selecting a program of study. Gather
information. The total solar eclipse on
December 4 suggests intriguing new
possibilities. Venus turns retrograde
near the Winter Solstice, impacting
your career sector through January 29.
Keep business and social activities separate during this time. Consideration

and tolerance are essential in your professional sphere. While celebrating the longest of nights release stale energies or troubling memories by doing a space clearing followed by some Feng Shui. As 2021 begins Mercury joins Saturn to favorably aspect your Sun. This enables you to combine traditional guidelines with new perspectives through the Full Moon on January 17. A supportive friend offers encouragement regarding a worthwhile project.

Late January finds Mars crossing your midheaven, a trend in force until March 6. You'll be highly visible and especially competitive. Pay attention to the impression you are creating. Put your best foot forward. A promotion, invitation or other opportunity is at stake. At Candlemas, on February 2, dedicate a candle to invoke goodwill and camaraderie. The Full Moon on February 16 highlights enjoyable hobbies and social interactions. A child's accomplishments can be a source of joy late in February.

February 17–March 9 try gleaning ideas during conversations or by following news programs. A favorable Mercury aspect in force then suggests spurts of valuable information which can support a cherished dream. As winter draws to a close, heed dream activity. Neptune is activated by the Sun in your 12th house of introspection. Intuition offers worthwhile solutions for resolving an ongoing issue which has been of concern to you.

HEALTH

Mercury has a powerful link to any health issues in your life. Talking through health concerns can often be helpful. Your birth sign has a special tie to the head. Always avoid eye strain and attend to eye health. It's important for you to downplay depressing situations and to maintain an optimistic outlook to assure well-being. The New Moon on September 6 is a wonderful time to address health habits and to begin a new fitness regime.

LOVE

Your love indicators are blessed with favorable influences from Venus, the celestial love goddess, March 21–April 14, June 27–July 20, and again October 7–November 5. Either a new love or existing relationship promises happiness then. While Venus is retrograde from late December through late January avoid socializing with colleagues. A workplace romance then could wreak havoc.

SPIRITUALITY

The eclipses on May 26 and December 4 directly affect spiritual experiences. Visiting sacred sites or attending spiritual services which explore new philosophical traditions from other lands can deepen spirituality near those times.

FINANCE

Uranus continues a long transit through your financial sector all year. Changing values, new worldwide economic trends and unexpected events will make finances rather unpredictable. The November 19 eclipse highlights the specifics. Avoid risky investments or overextending financially, especially during the winter months. Planetary cycles favor finances April 14–May 8 and September 12–October 6.

TAURUS
April 20–May 20
Spring 2021–Spring 2022 for those
born under the sign of the Bull

The Bull's outlook on life is steady with an earthy appreciation for creature comforts. Taurus has an affinity for nature which usually gives a legendary "green thumb." Your gardens and houseplants tend to be beautiful and lush. Through persistence, sometimes amounting to pure bull-headedness, Taurus will nearly always materialize desired goals and dreams. Fragrances, colors and sounds delight your sensual nature. Musical ability, especially in singing, is often among your talents.

From the Vernal Equinox through April 3 an upbeat 11th house Mercury influence prevails. Friends offer valuable information and invitations. This might involve travel. Mid-April brings a yearning for peace. Enjoy solitary reverie and meditation during the week of the New Moon on April 11. April 15–May 8 finds Venus, your ruler, conjunct your Sun. Create May Day baskets filled with spring flowers to offer at seasonal celebrations. From mid-May through June 22 financial planning is uppermost in your mind. The retrograde Mercury cycle then renews old business connections near the Summer Solstice.

As July begins Venus and Mars are moving through your sector of home, family and heritage. Residential improvements, devotion to family or planning a reunion are all likely possibilities. As Lammas nears Mercury and the Sun accent your family tree. Explore the geographical areas associated with your ancestry near the New Moon on August 8. Jupiter's retrograde cycle affects your professional status and public visibility throughout the remainder of August. Good work you've done in the past will be appreciated. During the first two weeks of September the Sun and Mars favor your sector of leisure time activities. An enjoyable vacation, recreation or hobbies brighten summer's final days.

At the Autumnal Equinox the Sun joins Mars in your 6th house, encouraging you to get organized. As a result you can complete an ongoing service project by late October. At All Hallows transits of Venus and Neptune encourage choosing a comfortable costume. Consider a boho chic or '70s look. November ushers in a spirit of challenge and competition. This is fueled by a strong Mars aspect. Avoid legal entanglements. Keep a sense of humor. Patience goes a long way in getting through a disagreement gracefully near the lunar eclipse in Taurus on November 19. At the end of November and beginning of December managing insurance coverage, an estate or investments captures your attention. The eclipse on December 4 favors fiscal flexibility. Observe current economic trends.

Venus is retrograde December 19–January 29, 2022. Your 9th house is affected. Relationships with in-laws as well as grandparent-grandchild dynamics can go through some fluctuations. A thoughtful gesture on your part would be helpful. At the Winter Solstice a Mercury-Uranus trine brings valuable insights. Listen carefully to casual remarks. The nuances in voices and the sounds of nature in the environment around you will have a way of deepening your understanding. As 2022 begins Jupiter changes signs. This accents community life. Your circle of acquaintances expands. New goals come into focus. The winter months bring an inclination to explore and learn.

Verify and double-check your work during the retrograde Mercury cycle January 14–February 4. Follow through with career obligations. Light a green or white taper at Candlemas for illumination regarding a financial decision. You might be preparing to leave a job by the end of February. The Full Moon on February 16 brings the emotional needs of family members into play. Keep calm if a relative appears to be overreacting to minor issues.

Venus, Mars and Pluto impact your 9th house March 1–5. All that is unfamiliar and exotic is appealing. Travel, reading, fresh and newsworthy ideas will hold your attention. This is a great cycle for learning or sharing something new. On March 6 Venus crosses your midheaven and moves toward a conjunction with Saturn. As winter draws to a close the extra effort you make to complete a demanding project will be appreciated. A colleague expresses faith and confidence in you. The Full Moon on March 18 brings opportunities to relax while enjoying a game or other leisure time activity.

HEALTH

A sensitivity to noise as well as a tendency toward sore throats or laryngitis can be at the root of health concerns. Your birth sign has rulership over the ears and neck area. July 22–August 29 finds celestial patterns enhancing your overall wellness. The week of the New Moon on September 6 favors making choices regarding your health care.

LOVE

Venus activates your first house April 15–May 8. Whether you enjoy an existing relationship or are receptive to a new romance, the stars indicate a happy interlude then. Uranus is in the midst of a long transit through your birth sign all year, bringing some sparkle and surprises as you explore relationships. The Venus retrograde December 19–January 29 offers a new perspective concerning a lost love from long ago.

SPIRITUALITY

Oftentimes spiritual awakening enters your life through sacred art and liturgical music. This year promises intense spiritual experiences during the autumn and winter. That's when Venus will join Pluto while passing through your sector of spirituality. November 5–March 4 is the significant time.

FINANCE

The eclipse on June 10 reveals changes regarding either the source of your income or your financial needs. Be flexible while considering new job prospects and working with your budget then. Collect a bag of crystals or assemble a sachet of herbs to attract prosperity at the Summer Solstice.

GEMINI
May 21–June 20
Spring 2021–Spring 2022 for those
born under the sign of the Twins

Restless and sociable Gemini is forever curious. Naturally intellectual, you are motivated to choose a lifestyle which accents learning experiences. Those born under the sign of the Twins are the zodiac's adaptable multitaskers. Whimsical and changeable, you always seek to escape the dull and monotonous. Those who connect with you will quickly realize that you are a complex being with many facets. Perpetual change is the only certainty with Gemini.

The Vernal Equinox arrives with a burst of energy. Impatient and competitive Mars races through your birth sign through April 22. You are fed up with a few situations and ready to establish a new status quo. March 21–April 3 the influence of Mercury, your ruler, encourages new career directions. The New Moon on April 11 presents options regarding long term goals and community projects.

By May Day Mercury, Venus and the Sun will join Uranus in your 12th house. Heed a dream or sudden inspiration; guidance comes from within. Venus transits Gemini May 9–31 bringing financial opportunities and pleasant social interludes. Accept and issue invitations. May 30–June 23 Mercury's retrograde in your 1st house reinforces habit patterns.

Remember to keep all promises and be reliable throughout June. At the Summer Solstice prepare a rite of release. Let go of all that you've outgrown and prepare to move forward.

July finds Venus and Mars emphasizing your 3rd house of communication and travel. Interesting messages arrive, and a new vehicle or other desirable method of transportation may appear. Travel is productive and enjoyable throughout the month. The New Moon on July 9 favorably affects cash flow. New income-producing opportunities can become available. Plan journeys during July and early August. Visit a sacred site at Lammas. From mid-August through September 10 Venus, the celestial love goddess, will trine your Sun. This promises pleasure and romance. Summer's waning days mark bright and happy times. Enjoy hobbies and recreation with loved ones.

As the Autumnal Equinox nears, seek insight through the Tarot or other divination techniques concerning career aspirations. The retrograde Mercury period September 27–October 18 accents the needs of children or other vulnerable people. Someone feels lost and might benefit from some extra attention and guidance. The New Moon on October 6 favors gathering seasonal decorations. Make an arrangement of autumn foliage for your altar or meditation corner. During the last three weeks of October Venus moves through your 7th house of relationships. A partner enjoys success. Offer appreciation and praise for the accomplishments of someone close to you. Halloween brings invitations to participate in an enjoyable celebration.

November finds the Sun, Mercury and Mars in your 6th house. A cherished animal companion brings comfort as the nights grow longer and the cold increases. Near the New Moon on November 4 a new pet might appear and join your household. Late November through December 13 the Sun and Mercury activate a flurry of opposing influences. Be a good listener. A well informed associate shares worthwhile solutions to problems. Official paperwork needs attention. The Full Moon in Gemini on December 18, near the Winter Solstice, resurrects memories of those who have passed away. Thoughts about the afterlife and reincarnation are recalled. On the longest of nights caring and concerned spirit world visitors can be felt hovering in the shadows.

2022 begins with Jupiter crossing your midheaven, bringing growth and expansion regarding your goals and professional aspirations. Update your job knowledge during January. Jupiter and Neptune drift into a conjunction as the winter moves along. Heeding your intuition will enhance success and bring a compliment. February 14–March 9 Mercury and Saturn favorably aspect your Sun. Travel and spiritual studies are productive at that time. The rest of the winter brings Venus and Mars together in Aquarius, your sister air sign. This promises a burst of heightened vitality and creative expression. Responsibilities ease. Your workload lightens.

HEALTH

Currently Pluto, ruler of your health sector, is in the midst of a long transiting quincunx aspect to your Sun. This underscores the impact that fate, in the form of heredity and environmental factors, has on your well-being. Examine the deeper causes behind health conditions. The eclipse in Gemini on June 10 offers attunement to the wellness and care of your body. October 30–December 12 is also an excellent time to become proactive in addressing any health goals.

LOVE

A joyful springtime romance is promised when Venus transits your Sun May 9–June 1. The eclipses on May 26 and December 4 both fall in your relationship sector. This promises surprises and changes in the status quo of a love connection. Support the dreams of one you love while allowing him or her ample freedom.

SPIRITUALITY

Your 9th house of spirituality is highlighted by Saturn and Jupiter transits this year. Explore new spiritual paths through travel and study. Dedication to spiritual practices will yield genuine progress. Heed and analyze dreams. The New Moon on February 1, the eve of Candlemas, is especially powerful for spiritual expansion. Light white and silver candles on February 1–2 to attract a helpful spirit guide or angel.

FINANCE

You revel in using clever strategy to make a game of managing finances. The lunar phases reflect the financial highs and lows in your pocketbook. Follow the Moon Calendar as a reference, noting how the new, full and quarter Moons show a pattern. This will help you to make profitable financial decisions.

CANCER
June 21 – July 22
Spring 2021 – Spring 2022 for those
born under the sign of the Crab

The sensitive and sentimental Moonchild is the zodiac's nurturer. With empathy and intuition you are present when needed to offer comfort and security to family, friends and coworkers alike. Establishing a secure home and preserving your heritage are top priorities. The Crab persists no matter what regarding the pursuit of important objectives. This determination usually is rewarded with success in reaching your goals.

From the Vernal Equinox through All Fools' Day Mercury joins Neptune to create a favorable 9th house aspect. Faraway lands intrigue you. It's time to sharpen foreign language skills in preparation for travel abroad. During the first two weeks of April Venus brightens your career sector. Express creativity and cultivate social connections to boost your professional position. April 23 – June 10 Mars transits your sign, bringing motivation and assertiveness. If you control anger and impatience much can be achieved. The Full Moon on April 26 is fortunate for love and romance. Share a moonlit stroll along the waterfront with your nearest and dearest as April ends. On May Day cheerful aspects involving your 11th house favor celebrating with friends. June ushers Venus into your sign.

Others appreciate your charm and beauty. You will feel welcome wherever you go. At the Summer Solstice consider hosting a seasonal celebration.

During July retrograde Jupiter in your section of philosophy and education finds you rethinking established beliefs. You might be inquisitive about new studies or spiritual practices. This is a wonderful cycle for finishing a degree or certification program or completing a manuscript for publication. The New Moon on July 9 is in your sign, bringing a four-week cycle of great productivity. At Lammastide Mars shifts to your 3rd house. Observe the holiday by dedicating a talisman to promote effective and calm communication. Throughout August neighbors or siblings can express concerns or make requests. Respond with diplomacy and be a good listener. The Full Moon on August 22 highlights concerns regarding shared assets and joint finances. A compromise might offer the best solution.

During September and October Mercury makes a long transit through your sector of home and family life. There could be news from a relative who has been out of touch. Consider planning a family reunion to observe the Autumnal Equinox. Assemble an album of nostalgic photos. Add anecdotes. Share these sentimental memories at an ancestral altar on Halloween. In November Mars transits your 5th house. A favorite hobby, sport or game can spark your enthusiasm. The focus is on planning vacation and leisure time activities. The lunar eclipse on November 19 brings changes in your social circle. New acquaintances appear. Others grow apart.

Mercury joins the Sun in your health sector November 24–December 13, encouraging wholesomeness. Study information regarding health care. Understanding the mind-body connection can be significant. As the Winter Solstice nears, Venus turns retrograde in your 7th house of relationships. A sense of déjà vu affects a close partnership. For good or ill, history is about to repeat itself regarding someone very close to you. A past life connection could be recognized or an old flame can be rekindled. Create an atmosphere of love and sincerity on the longest of nights. Add a subtle sprig of mistletoe to seasonal decorations to facilitate peace and harmony.

2022 begins with the celestial healer Jupiter changing signs. This is a long-term transit which gradually improves health and vitality. Insight arises regarding your life's purpose and development of your natural talents under the light of the Full Moon in Cancer on January 17. Late January finds Uranus completing its retrograde in your 11th house. Uncertainty involving friendships and activity in organizations is resolved. At Candlemas light a taper dedicated to unity and camaraderie. February finds Venus, Mercury, Pluto and Mars in direct motion in your 7th house. Teamwork and cooperation are the keys to maintaining peace and finding happiness all month long.

The New Moon on March 2 brings dreams of faraway places and a yearning for adventure. March 10–21 a favorable Sun-Mercury influence stimulates higher awareness and wider perspectives. A conflict is resolved.

HEALTH
The eclipses on May 26 and December 4 affect your health sector. Be aware of how you feel. Address any changes in your physical condition this year. Be gentle with yourself. Explore new wellness alternatives. Health is favored May 14–July 27 and January 1–March 20.

LOVE
Venus, the love indicator, is in accord with your birth sign June 2–26 and September 11–October 6. Relationship situations promise happiness then. While Venus opposes your Sun November 5–March 5, enjoy the success of and praise the accomplishments of a close partner.

SPIRITUALITY
The eclipse on June 10 in your 12th house promises a deepening of spiritual consciousness. Time spent alone in quiet contemplation can spark spiritual insights all year. Connecting with nature and wildlife can also be a catalyst for significant spiritual experiences.

FINANCE
Mid-June to mid-August there are promising influences in your 2nd house of cash flow. Pursue income producing opportunities then. Volatile transits in businesslike Capricorn oppose your Sun during the autumn and winter months. Be cautious about acting upon financial advice coming from others then. Patiently listen to your own hunches regarding monetary matters and all will be well.

LEO
July 23–August 22
Spring 2021–Spring 2022 for those
born under the sign of the Lion

Bright and shining as its ruler the Sun, the Lion of the zodiac is warm, flamboyant and dramatic. With contagious enthusiasm Leo attracts the attention and loyalty of others. Instinctively you know how to present yourself in order to play a starring role at the center of every party. Your creative skills and flair for leadership allow you to make the best of what life offers.

The Vernal Equinox arrives with favorable Sun and Venus influences. Toast the sunrise and welcome the new season. The Full Moon on March 28 affects your sector of transportation and communication. A short business trip connects you with a desirable person. Others support your ideas during April. On May Day several planets including Uranus gather at your midheaven. Expect some surprises. Keep a competitive situation civil and good humored. Honor the holiday with fragrant incense, perhaps sandalwood or bergamot.

Friends are supportive from early May through early June. Venus and Mercury highlight your sector of groups and goals. By the Summer Solstice you will become interested in new things. During July fiery Mars transits Leo. Much can be accomplished, but turn down the heat if you sense that others feel overwhelmed. At Lammastide gaze into a mirror by firelight. Reflect on your image. Plan your goals for the year to come. On August 8 finance is accented by the New Moon in Leo. A four-week cycle emphasizing your source of income and security issues begins. The Full Moon on August 22 favors addressing the financial needs of loved ones and dependents.

September 1–14 finds Mars affecting your cash flow. Control impulse spending and seek the best price when making expensive purchases. September 10–October 6 Venus brightens your sector of home life and family. Happy times are shared with relatives. Appreciate your heritage. At the Autumnal Equinox perform a house blessing and welcome visitors to share in a seasonal ritual. October 1–18 the retrograde cycles of Mercury and Jupiter will affect communication and partnerships. Verify plans. Seek clarity and practice tolerance if a casual remark is confusing or startling. Someone close to you may have a change of plans or decide to back out of a project. Let go and let live. Respect the choices of another and all will be well. At Halloween Mercury highlights your 3rd house of words and ideas. Share favorite poems and legends which honor the season. Neighbors or siblings might have a story to contribute. Select a costume which recalls a favorite film or novel.

Throughout November Mars squares your Sun. Pace yourself; there is much to do both at home and work. Repairs to a vehicle or dwelling might be needed.

The eclipse on November 19 reveals the specifics. A job change or move might be on the horizon as well. November 24–December 13 brings supportive cosmic influences involving Mercury and the Sun. Your creative ideas will come to the rescue and resolve a dilemma. This is also an excellent time to decorate for the winter holidays and review your gift list. A meditation for healing and dedication to wishes for wellness would be helpful at the Winter Solstice. Your health sector is active from mid-December through January. Select a healthy diet and follow a wholesome lifestyle during the first weeks of winter. The New Moon on January 2 accents current health trends.

By Candlemas the influences of Jupiter and Neptune stir your 8th house. Light a votive candle to honor those who visit from the spirit world. During February your understanding deepens concerning a perplexing situation or mystery. The Full Moon in Leo on February 16 brings insight concerning your role in a relationship. Another seeks your advice and leadership ability. March 1–5 the importance of beloved animals is underscored as Venus and Mars move with Pluto in your 6th house. A health condition could improve dramatically in early March. The final two weeks of winter emphasize your relationships. Cooperation and sharing are the keys to resolving differences. Seek balance. Approach a volatile situation with fairness.

HEALTH

Energetic Mars transits Leo June 11–July 29. You can feel motivated to exercise more. A boot camp-style workout program might be beneficial, just don't go to extremes. Venus makes a long transit through your health sector November 5–March 5. The healing quality of love and companionship can be a positive factor in facilitating wellness. Those closest to you will take an interest in your health care.

LOVE

The eclipses on May 26 and December 4 are both in your 5th house of romance. Your love life will be brightened by sparkle and surprises this year. A new phase within an existing relationship can begin or a new heartthrob might appear. June 27–July 20 and October 7–November 4 especially favor happiness in love.

SPIRITUALITY

The eclipse on June 10 affects your 12th house of innermost secrets, solitude and charity. Meditation and quiet time during the weeks before the Summer Solstice would heighten spirituality. Supporting and working with a charity you believe in can also bring spiritual solace.

FINANCE

Uranus is midway through a long transit in your 10th house of career and accomplishments. This can bring changes in your industry or profession. Be aware of what is new and trending in your field. July–September your earnings and cash flow arena is activated by several planetary transits, including Mercury and Mars. Seek new sources of income. Extra work can become available then.

VIRGO
August 23–September 22
Spring 2021–Spring 2022 for those
born under the sign of the Virgin

Organizing to bring order into the chaos of life is the mission of the analytical Virgo. You revel in all that is detailed, wholesome and practical. Ruled by Mercury, you often excel at communication. Devoted to any job you accept, you are a hard worker, determined to always do the best you can. Earthy Virgo has an affinity with animals and appreciates nature.

Select and repeat positive affirmations to celebrate the Vernal Equinox. The springtime is greeted with a Mercury opposition and a Mars square to your Sun. The mood is hectic and there can be some distractions. Simplify. Work things out step by step. By April 15 Venus joins Uranus to favorably aspect your Sun. Tensions lessen by the end of the month. A jolly friend offers good humored companionship. Celebrate May Day by purchasing a bouquet of flowers. During May your 11th house is highlighted by Mars. Social interaction accelerates. Helpful people suggest ideas for projects to pursue in the times ahead.

Retrograde Mercury affects your career during June. There can be some delays or uncertainty affecting your work. Finish a job that has been dragging on. Verify instructions and appointments.

The Summer Solstice brings a sense of completion and release. Venus accents quiet, good deeds July 1–21. Your sense of purpose is reinforced by time spent in contemplation. Both Mars and Venus cross into Virgo in late July. An especially active cycle commences. You will feel the need to be assertive and creative. At Lammastide dedicate ritual work to creating change. Mercury races through your 1st house August 11–29. You will make wonderful connections, impress others with your eloquence, and make good choices. Travel is rewarding. As September begins, your financial sector is highlighted. Your salable job skills are in demand. The New Moon in Virgo on September 6 motivates your resolve to make positive changes. Mid-September accents financial goals and making desired purchases. Your birthday promises a shopping trip. The Full Moon on September 20 highlights partnerships and loyalty issues. At the Autumnal Equinox join a group healing circle.

October finds Mercury retrograde in your sector of values and security. You will seek to balance financial needs with other kinds of wealth, the things money can't buy. Late October–November 4 brings a joyful Venus influence to brighten your home and family sector. A real estate transaction or a redecorating project is successful. The eclipse on November 19 reveals new priorities. An interest in travel, new studies or spiritual alternatives will captivate you. Imported foods and cultural traditions from around the world can be appealing choices for the winter holiday season. December 1–13 finds Mercury conjoining the Sun, with a focus on heritage and established family dynamics. The eclipse on December 4 intensifies this trend. A visit to an old home town, intense conversations with or about relatives, memorabilia such as old photos or letters bring appreciation for your ancestry.

By the Winter Solstice Venus is retrograde in your 5th house of love and pleasure. Holiday traditions assume new meanings. News arrives from acquaintances who have been out of touch. You'll realize you are growing in a different direction and will prefer to look toward the present and future. As 2022 begins powerful transits in the other earth signs, including Pluto and Uranus, bring you good vitality and inspiration. The New Moon on January 2 begins a month-long phase when you can enjoy esoteric studies, creative writing or arts and crafts to enrich the deep, long winter days.

Venus will complete its retrograde cycle by Candlemas. You will be able to reach a decision concerning love. Light a rose-colored candle to honor what is near and dear on February 2. The first three weeks of February bring a shift involving your 6th house of health, your favorite subject. Information about wellness, treatments for ongoing health conditions and the health of others can be of special interest. In March Jupiter is prominent in your 7th house. Be cooperative and diplomatic. The actions of others can be quite beneficial. The Full Moon in Virgo on March 18 brings a sense of acceptance and warm camaraderie.

HEALTH

Jupiter, the celestial healer, moves through your 6th house of health from the Spring Equinox to May 13 and again July 28–December 28. Health goals can be reached during those times. Small pets have a deep tie to your birth sign. The love and devotion of a special cat, dog, bunny, etc. can add to your well-being.

LOVE

This year Venus makes a long passage through your 5th house of love from November 5 to March 5. At that time old relationship issues or heartaches can be resolved. The foundation for a solid long-term love connection can be established or strengthened. Visit places of natural beauty such as parks and gardens with one you would woo to set the scene for love to grow.

SPIRITUALITY

Uranus hovers in your sector of spirituality all year. Exploring new beliefs will deepen your insights. This might include visiting new places of worship and meditation or learning about the spiritual practices of faraway places. The month of May and the week of the eclipse on November 19 highlight spiritual realizations.

FINANCE

The Full Moon on March 28 impacts your 2nd house of finances. Information about the money situation surfaces and security becomes an emotional issue. During October a strong Mars influence motivates you to work hard, resulting in financial gain. Early January promises a lessening of financial stresses.

LIBRA
September 23–October 23
Spring 2021–Spring 2022 for those
born under the sign of the Scales

Equilibrium and balance characterize the special charm and style of Venus-ruled Libra. You are forever seeking harmony and beauty in all things. Companionship, thoughtfulness and fairness are important keynotes. In a desire to always do what is right Libra can vacillate. Decision by indecision can often determine outcomes in key situations.

The week of the Vernal Equinox brings a Full Moon in Libra. You will attune emotionally to the spirit of spring. A favorable aspect from Mars brings energy, motivation and enthusiasm through April 22. By May Day your 8th house of mysteries and research is active. Ancient traditions linked to the maypole and May baskets can intrigue you. An entity from the spirit realm sends a comforting message of peace. May 9–June 1 a Venus transit in your 9th house brings an elevating spiritual influence through art and music. From early June through the Summer Solstice Mercury's retrograde cycle resurrects happy memories of school days and long ago summer holidays. Take note of dreams recalled during the shortest of nights.

July brings visibility regarding your professional life. Public speaking or a piece of writing could be involved. The week of the New Moon on July 9 reveals the specifics. By Lammastide Jupiter is retrograde in your 5th house of love and pleasure. Honor the early harvest with an artistic arrangement of seasonal flowers, fruits and breads to share at a celebration feast. August promises time to relax. Responsibilities can lessen to make way for vacation plans while Venus transits Libra August 16–September 10.

On September 15 a powerful Mars transit lasting until October 29 begins in your 1st house. You will feel the need to be more assertive about resolving an issue or concern. At the Autumnal Equinox seek guidance from the runes or Tarot. The New Moon in Libra on October 6 favors developing a plan of action. When Mercury goes direct on October 18 progress is made. Honor All Hallows by sharing stories, ideas and lore with a group of close friends.

The Sun, Mars and Mercury march through your 2nd house of money during November. Financial matters need attention. Careful budgeting and looking at options will help. The eclipse on November 19 underscores the impact external factors such as insurance, investments or another person might have on your personal finances. During December novel ideas, involving a change of scene and escape from redundancy will be appealing. A short journey near the eclipse on December 4 would be refreshing. As the Winter Solstice nears, Venus turns retrograde in your sector of home and family. A strong sentimental quality surfaces. Display some keepsake ornaments and prepare a favorite family recipe to serve at dinner on the longest of nights.

During January Jupiter's transit emphasizes getting organized. It's a good time to clear away clutter. A cherished animal companion is a source of solace and enjoyment. The Full Moon on January 17 brings insights into your options regarding career goals. By Candlemas Venus will have completed its retrograde. Dedicate yellow and white altar candles to the resolution of a sensitive family situation. Throughout February Mars squares your Sun. A competitive or stressful situation is brewing. Be grateful for all you have and resist the temptation to be envious of others. The Full Moon on February 16 brings encouragement from close friends. Set goals for the future in late February.

As March begins a Mercury-Saturn conjunction generates a favorable influence in your 5th house. The accomplishments of a child can be a source of joy. You might feel more serious about merging a hobby or leisure pursuit with your career path. March 6–21 brings trines from Venus and Mars to your Sun. Motivation increases. The support of loved ones encourages you to engage in a new venture.

HEALTH

Neptune has a link to your health sector. Getting enough sleep will always be important in staying well. Time spent near the waterfront can be revitalizing. Consider a seaside vacation or ocean cruise. A health concern takes a turn for the better December 29–March 20 when Jupiter advances in your health sector.

LOVE

You are a true romantic. Exchanging tokens of affection and greeting cards with one you care for reinforces important love connections. August 16–September 10 and March 6–20 bring fortunate Venus influences promising happiness in love. The Venus retrograde December 19–January 29 is a time to be casual and cautious in love. Cultivate friendship more than rushing into a committed situation. An encounter with a past love interest finds history repeating itself during the winter months.

SPIRITUALITY

An airy and mercurial quality characterizes your approach to spirituality. Keeping a journal to document your spiritual journey can always be helpful. The eclipse on June 10 occurs in your 9th house of spirituality. This promises a sudden and profound spiritual experience during the late spring or summertime. Travel or a new course of metaphysical study can play a part in this.

FINANCE

A dash of secrecy often surrounds your finances as Pluto rules your 2nd house of cash flow. Inherited or invested funds can supplement your earned income. There can be some old debts or other financial obligations to address this year. The Full Moon on April 26 offers insight into finances. That would be an optimum time to prepare a prosperity ritual. September 11–October 6 brings a promising transit of Venus through your financial sector with potential for gain.

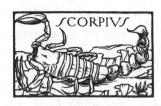

SCORPIO
October 24–November 21
Spring 2021–Spring 2022 for those
born under the sign of the Scorpion

Subtle and intense Scorpio is surrounded by an aura of mystery. Your intuition is sharp and so is your intellect. You conceal disappointment so as not to appear vulnerable. Ruled by inscrutable Pluto, there is a fascination with endings and beginnings, with transformation and hidden depths. The Scorpion's sense of perfect timing often leads to unexpected success.

The Vernal Equinox welcomes Mercury transiting your love and pleasure sector. Communication and travel plans shared with a loved one brighten the early spring. April 4–18 wellness is a focus. Several planets affect your health sector. Gather information and be open to trying new treatments to address any ongoing health concerns. The Full Moon in Scorpio on April 26 brings flashes of insight. Confusion is cleared. Pluto turns retrograde in your 3rd house on April 28. A long cycle begins which enables you to draw upon past experiences in order to make good choices.

The first week of May finds Venus opposing your Sun. Accept an invitation near May Day. Another is reaching out to you offering a new relationship. Late May to mid-June ushers in a supportive Mars trine to your Sun. Motivation is at a peak, allowing you to complete work in record time. During the last half of June the captivating cuisine and cultural influences of other lands inspire you. Incorporate an international mood into your Summer Solstice celebration.

July brings some stress into your work environment. Mars and Venus clash in your 10th house of status and visibility. Keep a sense of humor if dealing with someone who has an inflated ego. Make a humble effort to simply do your job and carry on. August begins with grounding influences from Uranus and Venus transits in earth signs. You will attune to the land. Add a potted plant and dark-colored crystals to a seasonal altar as you honor Lammastide. The New Moon on August 8 propels you into a position of leadership, setting the pace for the remainder of the month. September begins with Mercury activating your 12th house. You'll secretly feel a strong empathy toward those in need. Charitable efforts to help disadvantaged people or rescuing animals can be satisfying and bring you a sense of inner peace during summer's last weeks. At the Autumnal Equinox collect donations of food or household items to benefit those less fortunate.

October 7–November 3 brings encouraging monetary opportunities as Venus moves through your 2nd house of earning power and finance. A friend's recommendation can be helpful regarding your income. Dedicate All Hallows to a prosperity blessing. Honor and appreciate a legacy, whether it involves material goods or other less tangible gifts. The New Moon in Scorpio on November 4 conjoins Mars. You'll experience a new found sense of independence and an ability to meet challenges. In November you can make changes for the better. December 1–12 a Mars-Jupiter aspect affects your 1st and 4th houses. Different alternatives regarding housing and family dynamics emerge. In late December Venus turns retrograde. This affects your sector of communication, neighbors and siblings. Be tactful if someone's words or actions are upsetting. Detach. Distance yourself from anyone who is disagreeable. At the Winter Solstice a strong Saturn influence prevails. Bless a timepiece or calendar with thoughts about using the gift of time in the present and future.

By January of 2022 a benevolent Jupiter transit affects your 5th house of leisure and romance. Develop a creative idea, enjoy some recreation. A love relationship deepens while sharing mutually enjoyable activities. The Mercury retrograde of January 14–February 4 offers an opportunity to resolve disputes. At Candlemas light three silver candles to dissipate any hurt feelings stemming from thoughtless remarks. In mid-February the Sun, Mercury and Saturn gather in your 4th house. Commitments and promises involving family (or extended family) ties are the foundation for the future. Interaction between the different generations brings valuable perspectives to young and old alike. March 1–5 finds Venus and Mars gliding together to aspect your Sun. Focus on productivity. A business trip is worthwhile. Winter ends with the Sun, Neptune, Jupiter and Mercury all in a supportive cluster. Work is enjoyable and rewarding. A hunch, perhaps through a message received in a dream, guides you toward making wise choices.

HEALTH
In the spring a Venus transit spanning March 21–April 14 favors health care. Consider brewing a spring tonic or enrolling in a fitness program to augment good health at that time. The New Moon on April 11 promises changes for the better regarding wellness goals.

LOVE
The Venus transit through Scorpio points to love September 11–October 6. A relationship which can heal a past heartache is likely when Jupiter, the most fortunate of planets, moves through your 5th house of love. This occurs May 14–July 27 and again from December 29 through the end of winter.

SPIRITUALITY
The Moon rules your 9th house of spirituality. In esoteric astrology the Moon ties to the emotional recollections of the soul. Karmic or past life associations will characterize your spiritual experiences. Full and New Moon observances can boost spirituality. The lunar eclipse on November 19 and the Full Moon on December 18 especially promise spiritual awakening.

FINANCE
Two eclipses, on May 26 and December 4, are in your 2nd house, the sector of monetary gain. A new source of income might replace the status quo. Adapt to surprises. Changes in the economy can affect your line of work. June and January favor finances this year.

SAGITTARIUS
November 22–December 21
Spring 2022–Spring 2022 for those
born under the sign of the Archer

Life is a characterized by wanderlust for this Jupiter-ruled birth sign. An urge to grow and explore attracts you to a variety of different types of people and life experiences. Animal companions are important to Sagittarians. Freedom to travel to foreign places and to seek new challenges will appeal to you. Cheerful and fun-loving, you often inspire and encourage others.

Honor the Vernal Equinox with a blessing to facilitate cooperation. Mars opposes your Sun through April 22. Someone is a bit cranky or troubled. The New Moon on April 11 conjoins Venus and Mercury in your love sector. A fresh relationship perspective emerges then. Happiness is restored by the end of the month. On May Day a surprising Sun-Uranus conjunction affects your 6th house. A new animal companion might enter your life at a seasonal picnic or maypole dance. The remainder of May emphasizes health. Well organized and clean surroundings would do much to enhance your well-being.

During June, retrograde Mercury in your 7th house finds others anxious to communicate. Concentrate and listen in order to make beneficial choices.

Jupiter turns retrograde on June 19, just before the Summer Solstice. Customs and memories will highlight the remainder of the month. Plan a traditional celebration to honor the Sun on the longest of days. During the first three weeks of July your energy level will be high. Fire sign transits highlight your 9th house of travel and higher education. You'll be motivated to begin new studies or explore unfamiliar places. A Mercury trine to your Sun at Lammastide finds you sharing your adventures. Present and talk about your travel photos and souvenirs at a gathering in early August. After the Full Moon on August 22 career goals are of concern. A longtime job position is poised on the brink of change. Gather information and assemble a plan in case a move is needed. The specifics come into view September 1–14.

The Autumnal Equinox accents your sector of group participation and community life. Becoming more active within an organization would be worthwhile. September 27–October 18 retrograde Mercury brings news from an associate who has been out of touch. This revives your interest in pursuing a longtime goal or past project. By All Hallows Venus is in Sagittarius. Love connections, both past and present, spanning this world and the afterlife, will be trending. Feature games and costumes at Halloween. Decorate with laughing jack o' lanterns. November shifts the focus to your 12th house of privacy and introspection. You will cherish quiet time to focus on meditation and reflection. As the dark increases and the gloom time begins you might seek refuge in the wilderness. Enjoy a nature film or a hike to a visit a remote place of natural beauty. By November 24 the Sun and Mercury will enter your 1st house. You will be expressive and interact more with others. Your worthwhile suggestions and remarks initiate lively conversations. Make plans for a group ritual to celebrate the Winter Solstice. On December 13 Mars begins a transit through Sagittarius which sets the pace until January 23. Your enthusiasm will be contagious. Involvement in a favorite sport or game or dedication to a worthwhile cause can become a focus. During mid-January Uranus completes its retrograde in your health sector. This indicates a turn for the better regarding either your own health or that of a favorite pet.

Early February finds earth sign transits, including Mercury, Venus and Mars prominent. Candlemas is all about security issues. An ongoing financial concern can be resolved. Light deep green and black votive candles scented with pine or patchouli fragrances to attract and stabilize prosperity. The Full Moon on February 16 is in your 9th house of higher consciousness. This renews optimism and faith. You will develop a broader perspective which enables you to overcome a past disappointment. The New Moon on March 2 touches your 4th house of home, family and heritage, bringing a deeper empathy for relatives. A difference of opinion can be resolved. Real estate transactions are favored in March. A new home might offer a new lease on life as winter draws to a close.

HEALTH

The force of habit impacts your well-being. You have a strong fixed sign influence affecting your 6th house of health. Watch overindulgence. The eclipse on November 19 can bring new insights into how best to approach health care.

LOVE

Your 5th house of love is linked with fiery, impulsive Mars. You enjoy a challenge, even a competitive situation, in love. Romantic involvements tend to begin and end suddenly. March 21–April 14 and October 7–November 4 bring positive Venus transits which favor romance. The Full Moon on October 20 shines in your love sector. Dedicate ritual work to attracting a happy love at that time.

SPIRITUALITY

The eclipses on May 26 and December 4 are both in Sagittarius. This promises a year of profound, life-changing experiences. Your spiritual perceptions can shift before the year ends. Celebrations at the summer and winter solstices can be especially meaningful in exploring the meaning of spirituality.

FINANCE

Venus blesses your 2nd house of money November 5–March 5. This boosts financial gains. A creative idea or social connections can be profitable then. Jupiter's influence on your 4th house May 14–July 27 and again from December 30 through the winter months promises gain through a family member's generous contributions or financial connections.

CAPRICORN
December 22–January 19
Spring 2021–Spring 2022 for those
born under the sign of the Goat

Ruled by conscientious and reliable Saturn, Capricorn has the reputation of being quite a stoic character. The Goat climbs, survives and thrives amid challenges. However, a subtle, even a wicked sense of humor lurks beneath that solemn exterior. You have a terrific sense of timing and a dry wit which both surprises and charms others; once they catch on, that is. You're also good with money.

Venus welcomes the Vernal Equinox in your sector of residence. Schedule a good spring cleaning followed by a house blessing. Include edible arrangements of spring greens on your altar. The first half of April favors completing household repairs and a decorating project. On April 19 Mercury and the Sun join Uranus in your 5th house of romance. Conversations, perhaps punctuated by poetry, set the stage for love trysts. Surprise someone you care for on May Day with a visit to a beautiful garden. Attune to the nature spirits. Observe the fey ones as they tend the blossoms.

Throughout May and early June Mars opposes your Sun. A close partnership brings challenges. Control anger and impatience. Calmly try to understand underlying motives. Mercury is retrograde through June 23, bringing several changes in plans. Flexibility and communication help you to cope. At the Summer Solstice focus on clarity. Invoke the light of the Sun for guidance and inspiration. During July a strong 8th house influence brings a focus on shared assets, investments or an inheritance. Wise management is the key to attaining financial success. At Lammastide, the early harvest, express gratitude. August 1–15 welcomes a favorable Venus influence into your 9th house. Relationships with in-laws and grandchildren or grandparents are enjoyable. The foods, music and art of other lands are appealing during August. This is also a great time to travel abroad. Sharpen your foreign language skills.

During September your sector of accomplishment is accented by several transits, including Mercury and Mars. You'll feel motivated to begin demanding new work. There is a need to have realistic expectations of yourself. At the Autumnal Equinox apply the ancient Greek axiom "Know Thyself," calling upon the oracle of the Temple of Apollo at Delphi. The New Moon on October 6 begins a positive cycle linked to your professional status. On October 11 Saturn completes a retrograde cycle which started back in May. An old debt or other financial obligations have been met. You now begin to build a more secure foundation for your financial future. At All Hallows offer gold-wrapped chocolate coins as Halloween treats and invoke ancestral guidance for prosperity. Secretly tuck an antique gold or silver coin into your wallet as a lucky money charm.

November finds Venus entering your sign, affecting your 1st house until early

March. Your charisma level is on the rise. During the late autumn and winter months it will be easy to charm others with your pleasant demeanor. November 6–23 finds Mercury racing through your 11th house. Enjoy holiday season events arranged by organizations in which you're active.

December introduces a more reflective phase. A sensitivity to the problems of others or concerns regarding global events can draw you toward participation in charitable projects or other volunteer work. The eclipse on December 4 heightens this do-gooder trend. During the days before the Winter Solstice you will revel in solitary interludes. Guidance comes from within on the evening of the Winter Solstice. On the longest of nights gather with loved ones to share a traditional feast and wassail toast. From mid-December through New Year's Eve Mercury conjoins your Sun. Plan a winter's journey or enjoy exchanging special holiday phone calls, greeting cards and letters.

January begins with Jupiter joining Neptune in your 3rd house. Conversations lean toward spiritual studies. Try your expertise at reading the Tarot or runes. Write a wish list at the New Moon on January 2 to help materialize goals. Venus finishes its retrograde on January 29 leaving you happy regarding recent social connections. By Candlemas Mars is approaching a conjunction with your Sun. You will want to surge forward. This powerful transit is in force until early March. Embrace the energy by adding bright red candles to your altar.

Influences from the Sun and Saturn combine to impact your 2nd house of finances from mid-February to March. You will want to stockpile. Make purchases to add to your supplies. As the winter ends, Mercury joins Jupiter in your 3rd house of mobility and commuter travel. Transportation needs are met.

HEALTH

The eclipse of June 10 is in your wellness sector. June is a good time to address health concerns. New publications about staying well can be helpful then. Your vitality improves during January and February under an energizing influence from Mars.

LOVE

The eclipse on November 15 creates a stir in your 5th house of love. It's a year of surprises and revelations in love. Venus makes a long passage through Capricorn from November until early March. Happiness in romance is assured then.

SPIRITUALITY

Your sector of spiritual consciousness is especially affected by the late summer and early autumn energies. The poetry and legends inspired by the harvest season can awaken you to spiritual values. The Full Moon on March 18 highlights spirituality. Attending a Full Moon ceremony then would be enlightening.

FINANCE

Of all the zodiac signs you best understand how financial security contributes to overall health and happiness. Jupiter, the most beneficial planet of all, will transit your 2nd house of money July 28–December 28. Promising financial opportunities are presented then.

AQUARIUS
January 20–February 18
Spring 2021–Spring 2022 for those
born under the sign of the Water Bearer

The uninhibited Water Bearer, your symbol, pours generously from the jar which is forever full. Flowing outward is the stream touching the whole world with a fountain of thoughts, goodwill, curiosity and originality. You are an idealist and humanitarian with concerns which expand beyond the individual to focus on the welfare of society as a whole. You resist accepting advice, especially if it includes being controlled by the status quo. Instead you prefer to discover things for yourself.

An airy, breezy quality comes in with the early spring. Air sign transits aspect your Sun. This creative influence encourages celebrating the Vernal Equinox with an imaginative arts and crafts project. Your 3rd house is impacted by Venus April 1–18. Accept friendly invitations to travel with neighbors or siblings. A change of scene would be inspirational and uplifting. Plan a maypole dance or may basket exchange to celebrate May Day. Throughout May and early June Mars creates a stir in your zone of small companion animals. Cautiously make sure a new cat or other pet is a good fit in your household before committing to a permanent adoption.

During June a very upbeat Mercury transit affects your 5th house of recreation and vacation time. Since Mercury will be retrograde, a return journey to an old haunt might be a good option. A romantic interest from long ago can unexpectedly revive. The eclipse on June 10 accents novel hobbies, games or sports. The Summer Solstice supports health improvement. Celebrate the longest of days sunbathing. Enjoy the benefits and antiseptic qualities of the solar rays. Meanwhile let a pitcher of sun tea steep. Sip it at sunset.

During the first three weeks of July, Venus and Mars are in your 7th house, in an opposition aspect to your Sun. There could be a clash of egos. Avoid controversy near the Full Moon on July 23. At Lammastide your 8th house is influential. Karmic or past life situations are in evidence. Dedicate a seasonal celebration to a theme which touches on reincarnation. August 1–11 a strong Mercury influence encourages chatter. Be a good listener; there are grains of truth emerging which offer valuable information. On August 20, Uranus, your ruler, turns retrograde in your sector of real estate, home and heritage. A residential move is possible. A totally different type of dwelling or neighborhood might appeal to you. A surprise emerges involving the family tree as August ends.

Venus aspects the Sun favorably September 1–9. Beauty touches your life, perhaps through visiting a place connected with the arts and literature. Business and pleasure mix in your career sector when Venus crosses your midheaven September 10–October 6. Arrange congenial gatherings with colleagues in order to promote an atmosphere of camaraderie. Aquarians often befriend business associates. The Harvest Moon on September 20 evokes a sentimental quality which remains in effect through the Autumn Equinox. Assemble an album of photos with anecdotal captions to preserve happy memories of the past summer.

During October Jupiter and Saturn will both complete retrograde cycles. A barrier dissolves. At All Hallows gaze upon the vast night sky while preparing to honor the ancestors. November finds you juggling career goals and family ties. Transits of the Sun, Venus and Mars are all prominent in your career sector, but the eclipse on November 19 shifts the focus abruptly to home and family matters. Advice comes from a caring observer. You will be guided to make wise choices and focus what matters most by December 13.

By the Winter Solstice an upbeat Mars influence in your 11th house brings enthusiasm for forming a "bucket list" of goals and projects to pursue during the times to come. On the shortest of days gather in a warm and comfortable setting with friends to visualize the future. December concludes with Jupiter changing signs to enter your 2nd house of values and skills. Your abilities are in demand.

January is the perfect time to catch up on your reading, as Mercury enters Aquarius. The New Moon on February 1 conjoins Saturn. A consciousness of time management emerges. At Candlemas place a calendar or clock on your altar to bless time. Add a yellow candle for awareness. During February Mars and Venus will join Pluto in your 12th house. There are secrets you may prefer not to share and situations you would rather keep confidential near your birthday. On March 6 Venus moves into your 1st house where it will remain through winter's end. A beneficial new relationship becomes important in your life.

HEALTH
Mars transits your 6th house of health April 23–June 9, motivating you to act regarding fitness goals. This is good if you pace yourself. Don't push too hard. At the Full Moon on January 17 analyze the importance of hereditary health factors.

LOVE
The last three weeks of May and the Full Moon on February 16 are cycles which favor romance and intimacy. Venus remains in your 12th house November 5–March 5. This brings unique opportunities to express your love in a humanitarian vein, assisting those less fortunate.

SPIRITUALITY
September and October are the times which most favor spiritual awakening this year. The Full Moon on March 28 inspires you to share spiritual activities with a group.

FINANCE
Serious Saturn transits your birth sign all year. There is an intense focus on meeting financial needs. Patient effort will pay off. Jupiter conjoins Saturn March 20–May 13 and again July 27–December 28. This planetary combination promises profitable opportunities.

PISCES
February 19–March 20
Spring 2021–Spring 2022 for those
born under the sign of the Fish

The imaginative Piscean longs to swim away from the mundane and material world. Alternative realities and the unseen universe are more appealing to you. You are a talented idealist, dreamer and romantic. Like the pair of Fish, forever bound yet swimming in different directions, you are something of an escapist. With Neptune as the ruler, Pisces mirrors the deep and mysterious ocean. Much is always stirring beneath the surface.

At the Vernal Equinox Mercury and Neptune transit your 1st house making you sensitive to nuances. A séance near the Full Moon on March 28 could unveil helpful information. During April your financial zone is highlighted. Follow through with income-producing opportunities. A neighbor is an angel in your life, offering friendship and assistance April 15–30. Beautify your residence with flowers or plants May 1–8. Celebrate May Day with a garden party or picnic.

Venus touches home and family life May 9–31. A relative shares good news. Congenial visitors arrive, discussing vacation plans. The eclipses on May 26 and June 10 bring conflicts between career goals and home life. At the Summer Solstice Jupiter turns ret-rograde. Sentiment surges. Haunting memories surface. On the longest of days direct your thoughts toward the future. Release lingering regrets.

During July your 6th house of wellness is affected by Mars and Venus. Exercise will be appealing. You will be aware of the connection between caring for your appearance and your physical health. A spa visit and some new wardrobe items would be a wonderful investment near the New Moon on July 9. July 28–August 11 a Mercury transit accents appreciation for both domestic animals and wild creatures. Install a feeder to attract birds to photograph, draw or just observe. Adding to your aquarium or adopting a new pet can contribute to your happiness too. At Lammastide invoke animal totems during a stroll outdoors at sunset. From late August to mid-September several oppositions to your Sun indicate impact on your life involving the actions of others. Be cautious about making commitments or promises. A relationship might have to be reconsidered near the New Moon on September 6.

On September 15 Mars shifts to your 8th house. Research a nagging puzzle or mystery during summer's last days. At the Full Moon in Pisces on September 20 a sudden flash of insight brings clarity. On the Autumnal Equinox dedicate a ritual to truth and justice. October begins with Mercury retrograde in your sector of investments and assets. Examine patterns linked to expenses. Aim to reduce overhead or resolve a debt. On All Hallows Eve coworkers and friends celebrate with costumes and capers. Join in. The magic of the old ways is present amid contemporary times.

During November Mars joins the Sun in your 9th house of wanderlust and adventure. A new program of study, spiritual topics, or travel to explore a distant place is promising. You may suddenly outgrow an interest which was important previously. On December 1 Neptune completes its retrograde in your 1st house. This presents you with a stronger sense of purpose and direction during the winter holiday season. December 1–13 a Mercury influence in your career sector brings news about job prospects. A holiday party combines business with pleasure. Venus will be retrograde by the Winter Solstice, affecting your sector of social interaction. Bow out of a large gathering. A more intimate celebration on the longest of nights is preferable. On December 29 Jupiter enters your sign where it will remain through the end of winter. This fortunate transit draws a variety of positive opportunities your way. Health and financial goals will be easier to reach.

Mars transiting your midheaven January 1–23 stimulates career activity and makes you more enthused about work. There will be encouragement concerning your job from coworkers or loved ones. Develop a creative idea. At Candlemas your 12th house holds a Sun-Saturn influence. Dedicate a cream-colored pillar candle to resolve a situation of personal concern. Gather multicolored votive candles and invite friends to gather for a healing circle. Let them light their wish candles. February 15–March 9 Mercury's transit encourages discretion.

Respect the power of silence. Tactfully cope with controversy. As winter ends, a volunteer position or charity project can appeal to you.

HEALTH

Jupiter, the celestial healer, dips into your sign May 14–July 27 and returns with stronger momentum from December 29 through the end of the winter. Health improves then. Jupiter does rule expansion though. Control weight gain by monitoring your intake of high calorie foods.

LOVE

Romantic transits of passionate Mars and tender Venus highlight your 5th house of love during the springtime. A happy liaison can be established then. The Full Moon on January 17 marks the onset of another promising love cycle during the mid to late winter.

SPIRITUALITY

Focus on spiritual needs and questions while falling asleep. Upon waking, journal remembered dreams or the first thoughts which come to mind. Over time a picture of spiritual progress will emerge. September and October indicate spiritual growth this year.

FINANCE

Two eclipses this year, on May 26 and December 4, impact your 10th house of success and status. Changes regarding your profession can affect your income. Adapt to new developments to maintain a good income. At the end of the year Jupiter's influence promises growth and profits.

Sites of Awe

El Mercado de Juarez

JUST SOUTH of El Paso, Texas and on the other side of the Rio Grande river is Ciudad Juárez—a very busy Mexican city. In its historic center overlooking the city is the cathedral of Ciudad Juárez, with its tall twin towers.

It is hot. Very hot! I should have made this trip in the Winter, not in June.

Here in Juarez, I am told, you can find anything that your witchy and magical heart desires. But to find these things, you must visit the flea market, which is enormous and located on the edge of the city. I have directions to follow but all the signs are in Spanish, and now I just turned the wrong way.

It doesn't seem to matter. I know the market is somewhere northwest of where I am and it is pretty big—shouldn't be a problem running into it.

Oh, up ahead I see a lot of bright colors and some flags. That's it! The bright colors and flags turned out to be tenting. Meant to keep out the sun and separate the individual sellers, these tents all seem handmade from various fabrics.

After parking the car, I grabbed a couple of bags from the back seat and now I'm walking over to the market.

This is amazing—baskets, cloth, clay pots, food, spices, carved wooden figures, painted dishes, metal trays,

toys, primitive furniture and bright colors everywhere.

I've really only had one very specific thing in mind to purchase while I am here—a deck of fortune telling cards—and here they are, at the second booth I've come to. I see four different styles, but three of these are stylized playing card decks. Just one of them seems rather unique and truly a divination set of cards. Only 12 pesos! Handling the cards, they seem pretty thin but I don't care. I want these for the images, not the quality of the paper. I try haggling a bit because I understand that is what you are supposed to do here, and I want to fit in. I offered eight pesos. "No," she shakes her head. She looks disgusted with me. Oh no, I might have gone too low. "How about ten pesos?" I say in my very poor Spanish. The woman looks like I took a lollipop out of her son's mouth and shakes her head in the affirmative. I give her the ten pesos and move on to the next booth. Score! It is hot and getting hotter.

Moving on to the next booth, I can see lots of fine pottery—so many bright colors. But none of them strike my eye. I'll just keep going down this aisle, because it looks pretty easy to get lost in here and I want one way in and one way out.

Up ahead I see a table with candles. I want to check this out. What would a Witch need from a candle shop? I can't buy too much—it is too hot and candles will melt in the car. I'll just get a couple of black ones, just because. I ask for "*dos velas negras*," hoping that I said it right. The woman reaches under the table and gives me four candles. I think she thought I meant two pairs, as they are hand dipped and two are on one wick. I'll take these, but they look different from the ones on the table. Before I get a chance to figure out how to ask her why not the ones on the table, she looks at my pentacle ring and then says "*Quieres estas velas*." I'm pretty sure this means "You want these." So, I'll just accept them. Actually, they feel a little more powerful than the commercial ones on the table. I smile at the woman and she's already smiling back at me. I'm not asking her how much the candles cost. I'll just hold out my hand with money in it and let her take the price. She takes a very fair price for this magical find—just a couple of pesos.

I came here for the fun of it and for the fortune-telling cards, but I am now interested in finding a *colibri*—a type of divinatory bird. Oh, but now I see garlic. Here the magical garlic is called *ajo macho* (male garlic), and is said to be more powerful than any other herb to get rid of evil influences. I'll take a few bulbs with me. It's not very expensive, two bulbs for only one peso! I'm not sure if I can carry these across the border into the U.S., but I'll give it my best shot. I'm really excited to have found three things so far, and less than an hour has passed.

Here is another table selling the same fortune telling cards. The sign says eight pesos! I've been had! It must have been because the other booth was right at the entrance to the flea market. I should have known better. Not much money, but it is the fact that I was taken for a market ride that bothers me. Oh well, welcome to Mexican flea market haggling.

Anyway, I need to let this go because I am on the hunt for a colibri. I have heard of and researched the colibri for a few years now. This is a special type of hummingbird whose body is dried and very carefully wrapped in a colorful silk thread, which is wound around the body many times. To use the powers of the colibri, a prayer is spoken and the beak of the bird is held close to your ear. It is said that the bird will speak to you of the future. I'm asking everyone about this little bird and no one seems to understand what I am talking about. *"Colibri? Colibri? Tiene colibri?"* I'm asking everyone who will listen to me if they have one. Oh, finally someone knows what I am saying. Pointing down the aisle, she says *"En el lado derecho."* This I understand—on the right. *"Gracias, senora,"* I say with a smile on my face. After a very short walk I come to the tent where the colibri are laying on the table. I never would have guessed what these were if I wasn't looking for them. There are so many to choose from. I think that one of the three in front of me could be a good choice—the one on the left is a dark orange and yellow combination. The one in the center is mostly deep blue. The one on the right is red. My intuition tells me to only buy one. Less is more. I'm going to take the one in the middle. At 15 pesos, I consider this a bargain. I won't quibble about this price either. I pay the woman behind the table and she places the colibri into a bag and folds the top in the traditional triangular style, locking it closed so that it would not open should I drop it.

I'm very glad to have found these things, here at the Juarez flea market.

I'll head back to the car now. It is too hot and I would just like to get back to the hotel and look over these fascinating Mexican treasures.

Oh no—more cards, and only five pesos! Ugh. I have learned a valuable flea market lesson!

Some weeks later...

Upon returning home, the picture of Marie Laveau which hangs on the wall in my office called for the candles that I purchased in Mexico. I decided to place a small hook next to the picture and hang a pair of the candles there. I will save the other pair to be used many years in the future, for a very special purpose.

—ARMAND TABER

Witch Hunt, A Traveler's Guide to the Power and Persecution of the Witch
Kristen Sollée
ISBN-13: 978-1578636990
Weiser Books
$20.85

Kristen Sollée will raise the hair on the back of your arms and fill your heart with grief and wonder. *Witch Hunt, A Traveler's Guide to the Power and Persecution of the Witch* sets out to acknowledge and encounter victims of early modern Witch hunts by travelling to the physical sites of historical Witch executions in various countries and listening to the spirits that haunt them. Through seven countries and forty-five towns, she brings the reader along on a pilgrimage.

It is rare to find a work both historically honest and fully embracing of the mystical, and *Witch Hunt* is both. Sollée's scrupulous research and thoughtful commentary contextualize every site she visits, allowing the reader to enter meaningfully into the world of each executed person. Her writing is free of pretense, and she openly discusses the limits of verifiable knowledge about these incidents. In a square in France where she recounts the horror of an execution by fire, Sollée notes of the victim—the best known in the book—"there is so much about her that has been lost to time."

Each page is a portal, and as you slip into her world, Sollée will introduce you to the alluring Giovanna in Florence, the young boy Hans Morhaubt in Bamberg, the ever-defiant Joan of Arc in Rouen, and all the other victims—seductress and virgin, child and grandparent, guilty and innocent—that she encounters. She says she imagined the details of these figures that she paints, that she opened her heart at each site and allowed the place to fill her mind with what the past might have been. Sollée is both humble and rational, calling her process imagination, but it reads like a channeling. This is more than travel writing, more than a feminist or historical embrace of Witches past, more than a reimagined tragedy. *Witch Hunt* is a work of conjuring, and the result is magical.

Slavic Witchcraft: Old World Conjuring, Spells & Folklore
Natasha Helvin
ISBN-13: 978-1620558423
Destiny Books
$16.99

WHAT A PLEASANT surprise! One might be expecting plenty of paragraphs dedicated to theory and comparative mythology in this new offering from Destiny Books, with perhaps occasional litanies about the historical significance of certain practices of Eastern Europe. Instead, this book is very much a stuffed, working grimoire or Hoodoo-style cookbook. In many ways it reminded me of Hohman's *Long Lost Friend* but with a particularly Slavic focus. I was frankly flummoxed at the sheer number of chants, prayers and recipes within. Of the pages of the paperback I was given, a mere smattering of it are dedicated to the more theoretical musings of occult practice. The rest is brimming with spells, spells, spells.

The book feels very much like a deep dive into the charms and practices of Slavic Witchcraft, both beneficial and baneful. From hexing noisome coworkers and stealing the luck of others, to protecting oneself from curses while utilizing love and healing charms, Helvin's thin book is ostensibly opulent with orisons of all varieties.

The above is not to say that she shirks the responsibility of proper explanation, for Helvin will certainly go into more detail if the subject calls for it. For example, she gives a brilliant and heartfelt explanation of the rich symbolism associated with Kutya—a traditional Slavic food offering to the dead, made from grain, raisins and honey—as well as with other choice topics. But for the bulk, it is a simple, unadulterated, conjuring bonanza.

Looking for a quick charm to stop nasty rumors? Perhaps something a bit more banishy? This book's got a slew of clever ideas one can springboard from. In fact, I challenge any Witch worth their salt to not find an extremely useful hex or charm within *Slavic Witchcraft's* pages. Highly approved and recommended.

Paganism in Depth: A Polytheist Approach
John Beckett
ISBN-13: 978-0738760643
Llewellyn Publications
$18.99

QUITE A FEW magical practitioners, after years of study and practice, find themselves in a dreaded rut where many of their previous rites and rituals feel somewhat hollow. When the spirit lags and the words and gesticulations feel more chore than revel or revelation, it is best to seek inspiration from those who have trod the winding pathways for decades. In this vein, *Paganism in Depth* is one of those tomes which comes along breathing life into our Old Ways from the point of view of a veteran practitioner, reminding us of the infinite sources of inspiration which surround us.

A heavy amount of this book is dedicated to devotional practices toward one's chosen deities, and the wild, glorious aspects of nature they represent. Perhaps it may merely be an Emerson quote or two found within, but there is much about the profound joy of experiencing nature in this book which brings to mind the work of the Transcendentalists or naturalists like John Muir. There is an unpretentious love of the untamed places and the Ancient Gods that radiates throughout this surprisingly practical and back-to-basics manual of adoration and verdant sorcery. Thus, when Beckett says his practice rests on a "foundation of mighty ancestors," one can feel it in their bones.

A mature and informed look at Pagan practices, *Paganism in Depth* delves into the deeply healing and transformative nature of rites and rituals furthering a union with the Gods. Ultimately it is a dedicant's ideal workbook with a poetic soul at its heart.

Familiars in Witchcraft: Supernatural Guardians in the Magical Traditions of the World
Maja D'Aoust
ISBN-13: 978-1620558461
Destiny Books
$16.99

LIKE MANY modern occult authors, Maja D'Aoust has been studying and teaching alchemy, occultism and Witchcraft for quite some time, now. This reviewer first met her over a decade ago at Manly P. Hall's Philosophical Research Society, a gem of an institution nestled within the controlled madness of Los Angeles, not far from picturesque Griffith Park. At the time she was doing an in-depth study on the works of Paracelsus, and she instantly impressed me with her vast knowledge and ability to parse more complex theories into delectable brain morsels. Her most recent book, *Familiars in Witchcraft*, certainly follows suit.

A delightful survey of all things "familiar," D'Aoust takes the reader on a trip through the ebbs and flows of folklore and historical record into this bizarre and fascinating world. Much less about pets and far more about the mischievous shape-shifting spirits who have ensnared, fascinated and occasionally troubled magical practitioners throughout time, *Familiars in Witchcraft* lucidly interweaves the lore of dozens of disparate cultures into a colorful quilt, and then points out the threads most common to all. Maja writes with the sweeping knowledge of a historian, but with much less of the snooze factor usually associated with said moniker. She is also adept at packing a slim cover with a massive amount of information, each bit more fascinating than the last. So if the odd spirits who torment and treat with magick users are your fancy, no matter where your tradition may stem from, there should be plenty of tantalizing tidbits within.

As if the above weren't reason enough to recommend this title, it is also is replete with black and white photos of the author's original raw, symbolic, haunting and surreal artwork. Snap this one up if you can.

Liminal Spirits Oracle
Laura Tempest Zakroff
ISBN-13: 978-0-7387-6274-6
Lewellyn
$23.99

ORACULAR DECKS of cards are as common place as tarot these days. Pick a theme and you are more than likely to find such a deck well suited to your needs. Laura Tempest Zakroff has created an oracle that we are sure will satisfy the most discerning witch. Continuing on a theme that she often lectures on, Tempest takes us on a deep journey into liminal spaces by presenting to us the 42 spirits that inhabit *The Liminal Spirits Oracle*. She has chosen a cast of spirits that are not only personal to her but also have strong connections to mythology and Witchcraft.

There are many features of this deck and subject matter that make this oracle so appealing. The individual cards are each an exquisite artistic exploration of the esoteric subject being expounded. The ethereal, pithy quality to Tempest's artwork is in no way assuming or inaccessible. In fact, each card seems to beckon the user to embark on the journey of the card. For example, the scorching heat of the salamander card can be felt, the coolness of the rolling waves of the ocean card begs a frolic and mysterious eyes in the mugwort card stand ready to reveal the mysteries.

Another feature that sets this deck apart is the organization of the deck. While it is not unique to organize cards in groups, Tempest has given us groups that are far from oridinary. She has ordered her deck into eight groups: Rites, Places, Trees, Herbs, Wings, Fur Fauna, Artifacts and Scale, Slither & Swim. Each of these groups of five cards is a collection of spirits with a common concept. There are two cards, Gateway and Mushroom, that do not fit into a group. These two cards are concerned with the most liminal of spirits, the beginning and the end of cycles.

The book that accompanies the oracle is a good read in and of itself. Rather than providing a compact size image of each of the cards, the book shows each in full size and full color. Tempest has taken the time to meticulously explore each of the cards, encouraging the reader to explore further.

Tempest has taken the time to the explain the use of the oracle for meditation and self-transformation. In her own words, "The deck was crafted with the intention of being a tool to tap into liminal realms and commune with spirits." In a lengthy discussion of doing just this, Tempest uses clear language to walk both the novice and the adept through the practicality and spirit of these endeavors.

Unlike most books accompanying various decks, Tempest is refreshlingly honest about the use of the oracle for spell work. While it is a short section, the text gives the user a good starting point for spell work.

Lastly, Tempest walks us through the use of the cards as a system of divination. For this particular oracle, she recommends staying away from the single draw divination, leaning towards the multiple card systems. You won't find the Celtic Cross here. Instead, Tempest gives you the typical three card reading. Her five card draw is an interesting approach to divination.

All in all, this is a vibrant deck with a unique approach, and well worth investigation.

From a Witch's Mailbox

The spice of life

I've been interested in the use of herbs for a long time. How do I get started?—Submitted by Jack White

The use of herbs in your daily life and in your magic can be quite rewarding. Because the knowledge base of herbs is so vast, you may want to be begin by studying the herbs that are native to your geographical location. That being said, there are many, many books on the topic. You will find more on the topic of herbal remedies than on the magical uses. A good source of information that is an even mix is David Conway's The Magic of Herbs *published by* The Witches' Almanac *last year. Another good source for occult and temporal use of herbs is Culpeper's* Complete Herbal.

It's all just wyrd

What is the best source for buying and learning runes?—Submitted by Eileen Sanger

Runes are a great tool for divination. Firstly I suggest that you familiarize yourself with the different types of runes that are used for divination and meditation. While they are all related there is a bit of difference between the Elder Futhart, Younger Futhark and Anglo-Saxon runes. There are several excellent sources for learning the use of runes, as well as rune magic. For a primer I would suggest Edred Thorsson's At the Well of Wyrd. *While it is a short book, it is succinct and without artifice. I might also suggest Ralph Blum's* The Book of Runes *which includes a set of clay runes. As for buying runes there are wonderful homemade runesets that be found on sites like Etsy. If you are an arts and craft kind of person, making your own could be satisfying.*

This house is not clean

I moved into my house last year and have been seeing a ghost everyday since?—Submitted by Joel Massey

Before we get down the nuts and bolts of cleansing a home, I might ask if you have determined if this presence is a beneficial land spirit or a trapped spirit. You would not want to banish a spirit that belongs to the land and is a natural manifestation. If you determine it be a friendly land spirit, you might intuit a way to work with it so that it brings blessings into your hearth and home. Now, if this is a spirit that is trapped in the house or land because of an unfortunate death or because it has lost its way, you definitely want to release it. I would start by cleansing each room with a good salt water washing of the floors and smudging in each of the rooms. Once this is done, I would make sure that each window and each door leading out of the home was anointed with the salt water as well. Once you have determined that the home is well cleansed, I would put a mirror facing each of the doors leading to the outside. You might want to make this part of a monthly cleansing routine.

Robes of a different color

I'm new to practicing Wicca. Do I have to practice skylad or is wearing a robe okay?—Submitted by Gail Evans Post

Well then, this is indeed a question that comes up frequently among those who are taking their first steps into Wicca. The choice of wearing a robe or practicing ritual nudity (also known as skyclad) is wholly a personal choice. There are arguments on both sides that make sense. For those who practice skyclad we often hear that we come before the Gods without artifice. It is hard to be anything but yourself if you are standing before the Gods in your birthday suit. Another argument is that the magic will flow more easily without fabric hanging off the body. On the side of robes, the argument could be made that you are coming before the Gods in your best attire. Those in favor of robes would argue that it puts you in a nonmundane mindset and that robes do not hinder magic just like walls don't. In the end, your decision should be made on what makes you feel most comfortable.

Is it really elemental

What element does the Athame belong to? Is it a Fire or is it an Air tool?—Submitted by Sadie Burke

Ah the perenial question of assigning the tools to the elements. This is truly a sticky wicket. You see, depending on your approach, be it Wicca or Ceremonial Magic, your opinion will be different. For the most part the Athame or dagger is associated with the element of Fire in Ceremonial circles. The Athame is asso-caited with the will of the magician and as such the burning will is naturally associated with Fire. If you are coming at it from a Wiccan perspective, many will associate it with Air. While it is still associated it with the will, the thought is that the will is a mental process and all mental processies are associated with Air. The rub is anger is associated with Fire and melancholy is associated with Water. So the answer is that you will have decide this one based on how you view the will of the practitioner.

Let us hear from you, too

We love to hear from our readers. Letters should be sent with the writer's name (or just first name or initials), address, daytime phone number and email address, if available. Published material may be edited for clarity or length. All letters and emails will become the property of The Witches' Almanac Ltd. *and will not be returned. We regret that due to the volume of correspondence we cannot reply to all communications.*

The Witches' Almanac, Ltd.
P.O. Box 1292
Newport, RI 02840-9998
info@TheWitchesAlmanac.com
www.TheWitchesAlmanac.com

192

978-1-57863-699-0 · $21.95
Jacketed hardcover · 6 x 8.5 · 256 pp

"*Witch Hunt* is a real pleasure . . . extensive, well-written,
well-informed and good humored."
—**Ronald Hutton**, author of *The Witch*

"Sollée writes with a deep respect for those whose lives were lost in the name of
witchcraft, and a wide, wild love for those of us who see the modern resurgence of
the witch as a signpost for a better, freer future."
—**Pam Grossman**, author of *Waking the Witch*

"Offering glimpses of the often overlooked legacy of the witch, *Witch Hunt* will
transport you to distant lands where the witch once danced.
A must read for any witch."
—**Gabriela Herstik**, author of *Bewitching the Elements*

www.redwheelweiser.com · 800-423-7087 · orders@rwwbooks.com

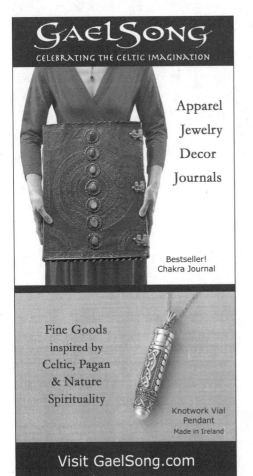

✺MARKETPLACE✺

Dikki-Jo Mullen

The Witches' Almanac Astrologer

PO Box 533024, Orlando, FL 32853

skymaiden@juno.com

http://dikkijomullen.wordpress.com

Seminars, Presentations, Convention Programs

Complete Astrology & Parapsychology Services

Paranormal Investigations

(see the website for astrology articles and information about upcoming events)

The New Alexandrian Libary

www.newalexandrianlibrary.com

The NAL is a library dedicated to the preservation of books, art, and the culture of the metaphysical and occult aspects of all religions and traditions.

Between The Worlds-Sacred Space Conference
April 9-12, 2020 • Hunt Valley, MD
www.sacredwheel.org/Conference2020
– A Fundraiser For The NAL –

The products and services offered above are paid advertisements.

The Witches' Almanac 2021 Wall Calendar

The ever popular Moon Calendar in each issue of The Witches' Almanac. is a wall calendar as well. Providing the standard Moon phases, channeled actions and an expanded version of the topic featured in the Moon Calendar are now available in a full-size wall calendar.

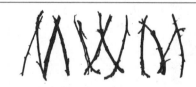

MARKETPLACE

www.AzureGreen.net Jewelry, Amulets, Incense, Oils, Herbs, Candles, Statuary, Gemstones, Ritual Items. Wholesale inquiries welcome.

The Crystal Fox 311 Main Street, Laurel, MD 20707 USA. The largest new age/metaphysical gift shop in the mid-Atlantic region. Monday-Saturday 10am-9pm Sunday 11am-7pm. **(301) 317-1980**, sterling@thecrystalfox.com, www.thecrystalfox.com

The Great Witch from The Seven Sisters of Salem Tarot cards, psychic, Spiritual Balance and Love Spells. Call Kathleena (773) 677 9247

Mardukite Truth Seeker Press Legendary books and tomes of magick by Joshua Free. Necronomicon Anunnaki Bible, Sorcerer's Handbook, Arcanum, Book of Pheryllt & more! mardukite.com NecroGate.com

Starwind Gifts Starwind Gifts, 5509 Magazine Street, New Orleans, LA 70115. Incense, candles, crystals, jewelry, cards, tarot & oracles, herbs, handmade soap, & services. (504) 595-9627 www.StarwindGifts.com

The products and services offered above are paid advertisements.

TO: The Witches' Almanac
P.O. Box 1292, Newport, RI 02840-9998
www.TheWitchesAlmanac.com

Name____

Address______________________________________

City______________________ State_______ Zip____________

E-mail_______________________________________

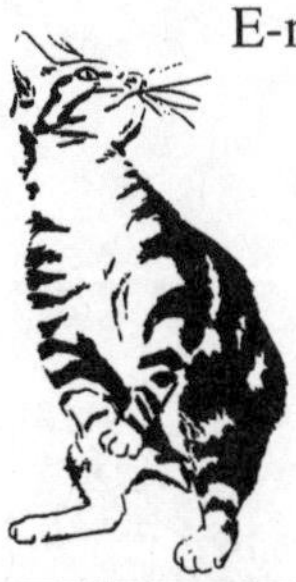

WITCHCRAFT being by nature one of the secretive arts, it may not be as easy to find us next year. If you'd like to make sure we know where you are, why don't you send us your name and address? You will certainly hear from us.

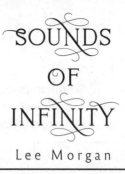

SOUNDS
OF
INFINITY

Lee Morgan

The Witches' Almanac presents:

• Faeries explored from a global perspective
• A poetic understanding and exploration of Faery
• A modern grimoire of Faery workings

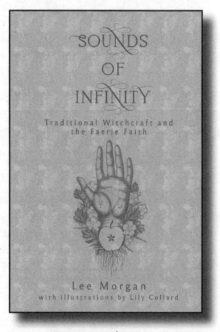

We are pleased to welcome Lee Morgan to our imprint. His latest tome, *Sounds of Infinity*, treats us to a comprehensive look at the world of Faery exploring geographical understanding, poetic understanding, and finally presents a very a workable grimoire. This book is about something so hidden it can never be the object of a direct gaze. For this reason this book aims to watch the faerie obliquely, off to the side a little, via a mixture of primary source study, ritual and art.

272 pages — $24.95

For further information visit TheWitchesAlmanac.com/SoundsofInfinity

THE MAGIC OF HERBS
David Conway

The Witches' Almanac presents:
- *Revised and updated with current understandings*
- *Explanations of herbal decotions, tinctures and poultices*

David Conway has revised and updated his seminal work, *The Magic of Herbs*. David was reared in a rural setting hecame to know about healing arts through practical application. 200 pages — $24.95

For further information visit TheWitchesmanac.com/MagicOfHerbs/

MAGIC: An Occult Primer
David Conway

The Witches' Almanac presents:
- *A clear, articulate presentation of magic in a workable format*
- *Updated text, graphics and appendices*
- *Foreword by Colin Wilson*

David Conway's *Magic: An Occult Primer* is a groundbreaking work that brought magical training to the every-magician in the early 70s. 384 pages — $24.95

For further information visit TheWitchesmanac.com/magic-an-occult-primer/

Harry M. Hyatt's Works on Hoodoo and Folklore:
A Full Reprint in 13 Volumes
Hoodoo—Conjuration—Witchcraft—Rootwork

THE WITCHES' ALMANAC is pleased to present Harry M. Hyatt's seminal work *Hoodoo—Conjuration—Witchcraft—Rootwork*. This masterwork of Hyatt's first published in five thick volumes during the years of 1970-1978 has long been near impossible to obtain. Working closely with Michael Edward Bell, Harry Hyatt's protégé, the collected field notes of Hyatt have been supplemented with his other major work on folklore, Folklore from Adams County Illinois. Additionally, to these very important volumes has been added Michael Edward Bell's comprehensive doctoral dissertation, Pattern, Structure, and Logic in Afro-American Hoodoo Performance (1980), which uses Hyatt's *Hoodoo—Conjuration—Witchcraft—Rootwork* as its main source. Bell's dissertation may also be used as a subject-index to Hyatt's five volumes. Hyatt had also prepared an album of 4 phonograph records (8 sides in all) containing most of an interview he had recorded with one of his informants, which we are also making it available as an mp3 file to purchasers of this reprint. The audio download is available at the time of purchase. Lastly, the purchaser will have online access to searchable files of *Hoodoo—Conjuration—Witchcraft—Rootwork*.

Harry M. Hyatt's Works on Hoodoo and Folklore:
A Full Reprint in 13 Volumes

Volume 1

Hoodoo—Conjuration—Witchcraft—Rootwork
Volume One
Part 1

Information:
- Page counts: "Each volume is approximately 500 pages in length."
- Number of Volumes - 13
- Book size: 8.5 x 11
- Audio files
- Ordering:
  email—sales@TheWitchesAlmanac.com
  voice—(401)847-3388
  visit—TheWitchesAlmanac.com/hyatt/
- Full Set (including audio download) $1,400

Aradia
Gospel of the Witches
Charles Godfrey Leland

ARADIA IS THE FIRST work in English in which witch-craft is portrayed as an underground old religion, surviving in secret from ancient Pagan times.

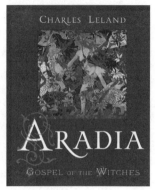

- Used as a core text by many modern Neo-Pagans.
- Foundation material containing traditional witchcraft practices
- This special edition features appreciations by such authors as Paul Huson, Raven Grimassi, Judika Illes, Michael Howard, Christopher Penczak, Myth Woodling, Christina Oakley Harrington, Patricia Della-Piana, Jimahl di Fiosa and Donald Weiser. A beautiful and compelling work, this edition is an up to date format, while keeping the text unchanged. 172 pages $16.95

The ABC of Magic Charms
Elizabeth Pepper

Mankind has sought protection from mysterious forces beyond mortal control. Humans have sought the help of animal, mineral, vegetable. The enlarged edition of *Magic Charms from A to Z*, guides us in calling on these forces. $12.95

The Little Book of Magical Creatures
Elizabeth Pepper and Barbara Stacy

AN UPDATE of the classic *Magical Creatures*, featuring Animals Tame, Animals Wild, Animals Fabulous—plus an added section of enchanting animal myths from other times, other places. *A must for all animal lovers.* $12.95

The Witchcraft of Dame Darrel of York
Charles Godfrey Leland, Introduction by Robert Mathiesen

A beautifully reproduced facsimile of the illuminated manuscript shedding light on the basis for a modern practice. A treasured by those practicing Pagans, as well as scholars.   Standard Hardcover $65.00 or Exclusive full leather bound, numbered and slipcased edition $145.00

DAME FORTUNE'S WHEEL TAROT: A PICTORIAL KEY
Paul Huson

Based upon Paul Huson's research in *Mystical Origins of the Tarot, Dame Fortune's Wheel Tarot* illustrates for the first time the earliest, traditional Tarot card interpretations as collected in the 1700s by Jean-Baptiste Alliette. In addition to detailed descriptions, full color reproductions of Huson's original designs for all 79 cards.

WITCHES ALL

A Treasury from past editions, is a collection from *The Witches' Almanac* publications of the past. Arranged by topics, the book, like the popular almanacs, is thought provoking and often spurs the reader on to a tangent leading to even greater discovery. It's perfect for study or casual reading,

GREEK GODS IN LOVE

Barbara Stacy casts a marvelously original eye on the beloved stories of Greek deities, replete with amorous oddities and escapades. We relish these tales in all their splendor and antic humor, and offer an inspired storyteller's fresh version of the old, old mythical magic.

MAGIC CHARMS FROM A TO Z

A treasury of amulets, talismans, fetishes and other lucky objects compiled by the staff of *The Witches' Almanac*. An invaluable guide for all who respond to the call of mystery and enchantment.

LOVE CHARMS

Love has many forms, many aspects. Ceremonies performed in witchcraft celebrate the joy and the blessings of love. Here is a collection of love charms to use now and ever after.

MAGICAL CREATURES

Mystic tradition grants pride of place to many members of the animal kingdom. Some share our life. Others live wild and free. Still others never lived at all, springing instead from the remarkable power of human imagination.

ANCIENT ROMAN HOLIDAYS

The glory that was Rome awaits you in Barbara Stacy's classic presentation of a festive year in Pagan times. Here are the gods and goddesses as the Romans conceived them, accompanied by the annual rites performed in their worship. Scholarly, lighthearted – a rare combination.

CELTIC TREE MAGIC

Robert Graves in *The White Goddess* writes of the significance of trees in the old Celtic lore. *Celtic Tree Magic* is an investigation of the sacred trees in the remarkable Beth-Luis-Nion alphabet and their role in folklore, poetry and mysticism.

MOON LORE

As both the largest and the brightest object in the night sky, and the only one to appear in phases, the Moon has been a rich source of myth for as long as there have been mythmakers.

MAGIC SPELLS
AND INCANTATIONS

Words have magic power. Their sound, spoken or sung, has ever been a part of mystic ritual. From ancient Egypt to the present, those who practice the art of enchantment have drawn inspiration from a treasury of thoughts and themes passed down through the ages.

LOVE FEASTS

Creating meals to share with the one you love can be a sacred ceremony in itself. With the Witch in mind, culinary adept Christine Fox offers magical menus and recipes for every month in the year.

RANDOM RECOLLECTIONS
II, III, IV

Pages culled from the original (no longer available) issues of *The Witches' Almanac,* published annually throughout the 1970s, are now available in a series of tasteful booklets. A treasure for those who missed us the first time around, keepsakes for those who remember.

Order Form

Each timeless edition of *The Witches' Almanac* is unique.
Limited numbers of previous years' editions are available.

Item	Price	Qty.	Total
2021-2022 The Witches' Almanac – The Sun: Rays of Hope	$12.95		
2020-2021 The Witches' Almanac – Stones: The Foundation of Earth	$12.95		
2019-2020 The Witches' Almanac – Animals: Friends & Familiars	$12.95		
2018-2019 The Witches' Almanac – The Magic of Plants	$12.95		
2017-2018 The Witches' Almanac – Water: Our Primal Source	$12.95		
2016-2017 The Witches' Almanac – Air: the Breath of Life	$12.95		
2015-2016 The Witches' Almanac – Fire:, the Transformer	$12.95		
2014-2015 The Witches' Almanac – Mystic Earth	$12.95		
2013-2014 The Witches' Almanac – Wisdom of the Moon	$11.95		
2012-2013 The Witches' Almanac – Radiance of the Sun	$11.95		
2011-2012 The Witches' Almanac – Stones, Powers of Earth	$11.95		
2010-2011 The Witches' Almanac – Animals Great & Small	$11.95		
2009-2010 The Witches' Almanac – Plants & Healing Herbs	$11.95		
2008-2009 The Witches' Almanac – Divination & Prophecy	$10.95		
2007-2008 The Witches' Almanac – The Element of Water	$9.95		
2003, 2004, 2005, 2006 issues of The Witches' Almanac	$8.95		
1999, 2000, 2001, 2002 issues of The Witches' Almanac	$7.95		
1995, 1996, 1997, 1998 issues of The Witches' Almanac	$6.95		
1993, 1994 issues of The Witches' Almanac	$5.95		
SALE: Bundle I—8 Almanac back issues (1991, 1993–1999) with free book bag	$ 50.00		
Bundle II— 10 Almanac back issues (2000–2009) with free book bag	$65.00		
Bundle III—10 Almanac back issues (2010–2019) with free book bag	$100.00		
Bundle IV—28 Almanac back issues (1991, 1993–2019) with free book bag	$195.00		
Dame Fortune's Wheel Tarot: A Pictorial Key	$19.95		
Magic: An Occult Primer	$24.95		
The Witches' Almanac Coloring Book	$12.00		
The Witchcraft of Dame Darrel of York, clothbound, signed and numbered, in slip case	$85.00		
The Witchcraft of Dame Darrel of York, leatherbound, signed and numbered, in slip case	$145.00		
Aradia or The Gospel of the Witches	$16.95		
The Horned Shepherd	$16.95		
The ABC of Magic Charms	$12.95		
The Little Book of Magical Creatures	$12.95		
Greek Gods in Love	$15.95		
Witches All	$13.95		
Ancient Roman Holidays	$6.95		
Celtic Tree Magic	$7.95		
Love Charms	$6.95		
Love Feasts	$6.95		
Magic Charms from A to Z	$12.95		

Item	Price	Qty.	Total
Magical Creatures	$12.95		
Magic Spells and Incantations	$12.95		
Moon Lore	$7.95		
Random Recollections II, III or IV (circle your choices)	$3.95		
The Rede of the Wiccae – Hardcover	$49.95		
The Rede of the Wiccae – Softcover	$22.95		
Keepers of the Flame	$20.95		
Sounds of Infinity	$24.95		
The Magic of Herbs	$24.95		
Harry M. Hyatt's Works on Hoodoo and Folklore: A Full Reprint in 13 Volumes (including audio download) *Hoodoo—Conjuration—Witchcraft—Rootwork*	$1,400.00		
Subtotal			
Tax *(7% sales tax for RI customers)*			
Shipping & Handling *(See shipping rates section)*			
TOTAL			

MISCELLANY			
Item	**Price**	**QTY.**	**Total**
Pouch	$3.95		
Natural/Black Book Bag	$17.95		
Red/Black Book Bag	$17.95		
Hooded Sweatshirt, Blk	$30.00		
Hooded Sweatshirt, Red	$30.00		
L-Sleeve T, Black	$15.00		
L-Sleeve T, Red	$15.00		
S-Sleeve T, Black/W	$15.00		
S-Sleeve T, Black/R	$15.00		
S-Sleeve T, Dk H/R	$15.00		
S-Sleeve T, Dk H/W	$15.00		

MISCELLANY			
Item	**Price**	**QTY.**	**Total**
S-Sleeve T, Red/B	$15.00		
S-Sleeve T, Ash/R	$15.00		
S-Sleeve T, Purple/W	$15.00		
Postcards – set of 12	$3.00		
Bookmarks – set of 12	$12.00		
Magnets – set of 3	$1.50		
Promo Pack	$7.00		
Subtotal			
Tax (7% for RI Customers)			
Shipping and Handling			
Total			

SHIPPING & HANDLING CHARGES

BOOKS: One book, add $5.95. Each additional book add $1.50.

POUCH: One pouch, $3.95. Each additional pouch add $1.50.

BOOKBAGS: $5.95 per bookbag. **BRACELETS:** $3.95 per bracelet.

Send a check or money order payable in U. S. funds or credit card details to:

The Witches' Almanac, Ltd., PO Box 1292, Newport, RI 02840-9998

(401) 847-3388 (phone) • (888) 897-3388 (fax)
Email: info@TheWitchesAlmanac.com • www.TheWitchesAlmanac.com